FRANCE

A FEAST OF FOOD AND WINE

France: A Feast of Food and Wine

Edited and designed by
Mitchell Beazley International
part of Reed Consumer Books Ltd
Michelin House, 81 Fulham Road
London SW3 6RB

This edition published in 1993 exclusively for
Marks and Spencer p.l.c.
Baker Street, London, England
T27 2634/4008

A CIP catalogue record for this book is available from the British Library

ISBN 1 85732 081 6

Typeset in Gill Sans, Sabon
Origination by Mandarin Offset, Singapore
Produced by Mandarin Offset
Printed and bound in Hong Kong

FRANCE

A FEAST OF FOOD AND WINE

ROGER VOSS

PHOTOGRAPHY BY JOE CORNISH AND RICHARD McCONNELL

St Michael

Specialist Food Shops in Great Britain

London

Bentalls of Kingston, Kingston-upon-Thames, Surrey KT1 1TX
Harvey Nichols, Knightsbridge, London SW1
James of Beckenham, 188 High Street, Beckenham, Kent BR3 1EN
Jeroboams Wine and Cheese Shop, 24 Bute Street, London SW7
and 51 Elizabeth Street, London SW1
Paxton & Whitfield, 93 Jermyn Street, London SW1
Selfridges, Oxford Street, London W1
Villandry, 89 Marylebone High Street, London W1N 3DE
Vivians, 2 Worple Way, Richmond, Surrey TW10 6DF

Avon

The Fine Cheese Co., 29 Walcot Street, Bath BA1 5BN

Cheshire

Godfrey Williams & Son, The Square, Sandbach, Cheshire CW11 0AP

Cleveland

Tom Walker & Sons, Thorpe Leazes Road, Stockton-on-Tees

Cornwall

Steins Delicatessen, 8 Middle Street, Padstow, Cornwall

County Durham

Partners, 26 Horsemarket, Barnard Castle, Co. Durham

Derbyshire

Pugsons of Buxton, Cliff House, Terrace Road, Buxton, Derbyshire

Gloucestershire

No 1 Food Halls, 3 Market Place, Cirencester, Glos.

Hampshire

Harvest Deli, 46 Main Street, Alresford, Hants.

Hereford and Worcester

The Mousetrap, 3 School Lane, Leominster, Herefordshire HR6 8AA
and 1 Bewell Square, Hereford

Lancashire

The Ramsbottom Victuallers, 16-18 Market Place, Ramsbottom, Bury, Lancs.

North Yorkshire

Lewis and Cooper, 92 High Street, Northallerton, N. Yorks. DU17 8PP
The Farm Dairy, 3 Market Place, Knaresborough, N. Yorks. HG5 8AL
The Queens Kitchen, 2 Queens Court, Main Street, Bingley, N. Yorks. BD16 2LT

Nottinghamshire

Cheese Cuisine, 10 Saracens Head Yard, Newark-on-Trent, Notts. NG24 1XA

Oxfordshire

Wells Stores, 29 Stert Street, Abingdon, Oxon.

Shropshire

Westry Roberts & Co, The Tithebarn, London Road, Whitchurch, Shrops.

South Yorkshire

Silver Hay Dairy, Eccleshall Road South, Sheffield S11 9PH

Suffolk

The Cheese Shop, 74 Beccles Road, Oulton Broads, Lowestoft, Suffolk NR33 8QY

Surrey

La Charcuterie Delicatessen, High Street, Cranleigh, Surrey GU6 8H7

Sussex

The Cheese Shop, 17 Kensington Gardens, Brighton, Sussex BN1 4AL
The Horsham Cheese Shop, 20 Carfax, Horsham, East Sussex

Scotland

Epicurus Delicatessen, 9 Leopald Street, Nairn
Garrard John, West End, Gullane, East Lothian
Jenners, Princes Street, Edinburgh
Kelly of Cutts, 345 North Deeside Road, Cutts, Aberdeen

Wales

Deli Delights, Black Lion Mews, Cardigan, Dyfed
Huxleys Cheese Co., 37-39 Birchgrove Road, Birchgrove, Cardiff

CONTENTS

WINE REGIONS OF FRANCE

INTRODUCTION

Trying to isolate how a book starts, where the first germ of an idea comes from, is sometimes virtually impossible. Ideas grow, they develop, and only after much germination do they bear fruit. It was almost the same with this book, but I think I can pinpoint one incident that, in retrospect at least, is where it began.

Many years ago, when I visited Bordeaux for the first time, I went to the village of Barsac, joint home with neighbouring Sauternes of great, sweet white wines. I was invited to lunch at one of the châteaux and there, also for the first time, I met the intoxicating combination of *foie gras* and sweet wine, offered to me at the beginning of the meal. I had always assumed – as most northern Europeans still do – that such wines are supposed to accompany dessert. This new view of their place in the meal was an eye-opener and a palate arouser: a chance to understand that the way we enjoy the great French wines is not necessarily the way they are enjoyed on their home territory.

Travelling back to France regularly since then, and exploring wine regions on most of those visits, it was inevitable that other combinations of food and wine – both classic and innovative – should appear on plates and in glasses in front of me, though perhaps not all on such a high plane as the *foie gras* and Barsac.

Some experiences were less than positive – I found that many French cheeses and red wine are inimical to each other – but others were truly inspiring: such as the discovery that mature white wines and goats' milk cheeses make perfect table-mates, that certain red wines complement the texture and taste of fish better than whites, that the rosé wines of Provence are natural companions for the oil and garlic used so liberally in the region's cooking.

Gradually, as these experiences accumulated, it became obvious that not only do the French have a different, and often more natural, more spontaneous, way of combining food with wine, but also that, in the wine regions themselves, local dishes and local wines very often appear to be made for each other. To look at the two together rather than, as most other books, to treat them separately, would, I felt, be a way of recording these effective partnerships, and of offering a more rounded picture of France's wine regions.

With this in mind, the following pages not only describe a very personal tour of France, where dishes are sampled impromptu at cafés and farms, or specially sought out from expert cooks, but each chapter also devotes a section to discussing some of the region's most characteristic dishes – ones whose historical place in the cuisine is essential to the whole flavour of the region – and for each a wine has been chosen to accompany it. These are combinations to try whether the dishes are encountered in France or further afield.

There were some ribald comments among my friends as I announced this latest project: "Off to France again?" and "How's the waistline?" were the politest – and, although I will admit to loving every minute of it, I will also admit that eating and drinking your way round France is neither kind to your liver nor to your weight.

But, at the same time, my eyes were opened to parts of the country I had never before been able to visit, or had sped through *en route* from one wine producer to another. I had the chance to appreciate the beauty, the size and the variety of the largest country in Europe, its emptiness and yet its richness – found in the pronounced individuality of each of the regions.

To travel from the cool of Alsace and Champagne in the north to the brilliant warmth of the Midi and Provence in the south, is to move from one culture to another – a progress that is today still clearly expressed in regional food, in a way that smaller countries such as Britain, or even larger countries like the United States, have all but lost, as much through indifference as through the proliferation of national supermarket chains and fast-food restaurants.

▲ *A place for conversation and relaxing outdoors, and the envy of travellers from colder climes.*

It may not be true that the French live entirely for their next meal, but, even today, when a lunch hour in many big cities is just that, and means eating a sandwich while desk-bound, the French still thoroughly enjoy talking about food, discussing the various ways a dish can be cooked, who sells the best pastries or charcuterie, and who makes the finest cheese. No doubt it has much to do with the French belief in preserving, and celebrating, their culture – something, surely, to be applauded.

I met many, many people on my journeys into hidden valleys, up remote mountainsides and around bustling towns; all of them were charming, thanking me for visiting them, accepting my idiosyncratic French with grace and understanding. And my sojourn into the French countryside taught me two things. First, that it is gradually losing its life-force: the people who work and live there. They are leaving the villages to find work and settle in the towns; the centre of village life – the café, the butcher, the baker – has gone out of business, leaving the community without a heart, and it is only in the small towns that these shops can survive.

And yet I found that amongst those who remain – and those who arrive – those who produce, grow and cook the food described in this book, there are people who give the feeling that all will not be lost if they can survive, and even prosper. They have a love, a passion, for what they do that goes far beyond simple commercial interest. Let us hope that they can sustain their way of life until the wheel of fashion turns full circle, and the countryside revives again.

The people who have helped me in researching this book are legion. Many are mentioned in the following pages and I hope they will appreciate what I have written about them, and be understanding of mistakes I may have made. But there were also many people, behind the scenes, who organised visits, made contacts for me or provided a bed for the night.

In Alsace, Oliver and Anne Humbrecht of Domaine Zind-Humbrecht helped in all these ways, not only making my research all the more enjoyable, but also letting me taste their first-class wines. In Burgundy I was helped by Anthony Byrne, British wine merchant, who arranged a number of visits for me, and by Gérard Salmon of Henri de Villamont, who generously offered accommodation at his firm's guest house.

In Bordeaux nothing could have happened without the marvellous support of Charles Eve MW of Château Loudenne, who opened the kitchens of the château to me, allowed me to stay in great luxury and arranged the fascinating excursions. In the south of France, help came from Mme Claude Vialade-Salvagnac of Château Saint-Auriol in Corbières, who gave me the chance to meet some of the most remarkable personalities in the book, while my time in Provence was organized with great charm and care by Joseph and Eva Berkmann in Saint-Tropez and Olivier Ott of Domaines Ott.

For my visit to the Loire I owe many thanks to the Comité Interprofessionnel des Vins de Nantes, to Jean-Paul Durie of the local tourism committee of the Loire-Atlantique département and, especially, to Charles and Philippa Sydney, courtiers in wines, in Touraine. They allowed me to stay *en famille*, rather than in a hotel, and put me in touch with so many people. Finally, in Champagne, I had enormous help from the Comité Interprofessionnel des Vins de Champagne, generally, and, in particular, from Philippe Le Tixerant and Marie-Pierre Locret.

To everybody I've named and to the many I have, regrettably, not had space to mention, my thanks for bringing this book to fruition.

ROGER VOSS

► *The pattern of life in France: a country where all lines converge on the vine.*

ALSACE

If you looked on national boundaries as immutable – as strict dividing lines separating cultures, wines, cuisines – Alsace would be in a state of perpetual confusion. The French tricolour flies alongside the gold stars of Europe outside every town hall, but these same villages boast names that would be more at home on the east bank of the Rhine than the west: Rorschwihr, Bergholtz, Kientzheim. And when talking to the local people, you quite often discover that French is their second language, after their own local dialect – either the one for northern or the one for southern Alsace – which to most foreign ears definitely sounds more Germanic than French.

Alsace skirts the German border in northeastern France – sheltered on the one side by the Vosges Mountains, bordered on the other by the Rhine Valley. This apparent dichotomy between German and French influence permeates the region. In true Germanic fashion, you don't eat lightly in Alsace – the piercingly cold winters, and the attendant need to stoke up on food as fuel, make central Europe feel very close. Plates are piled high with *spätzle* (small dumplings), saveloys and sauerkraut, every joint of meat and every vegetable is put to good use, dishes are designed for solid, prudent living.

And yet, as I sat in Jean-Marie Stoeckel's restaurant in Bergheim (a stone and timber village in the very centre of Alsace) watching dish after dish appear, I found myself applauding an almost effortless marriage of German solidity and heartiness with sheer French elegance. The very name, Wistub du Sommelier, joins two cultures: *wistub* is an Alsacien word meaning "wine bar" (*weinstub* in German); a *sommelier,* or wine waiter, is a peculiarly French institution. Traditionally, a *sommelier* worked in a large household and was expected to choose appropriate wines to accompany each meal; M Stoeckel, who was Meilleur Sommelier of France in the 1970s, is the ideal person to explain the idiosyncrasies of Alsacien cuisine and relate the region's cooking to its wines.

I had chosen a suitably cross-culture dish: *cuisse de canard confite sur choucroute*, roast duck on a bed of finely shredded, salted and fermented cabbage. For many, *choucroute*, or sauerkraut, is the archetypal Alsacien dish, but I had in mind the often quite sharp tang of German sauerkraut – a speciality of Bavaria and the Black Forest, and best accompanied in my experience with beer. "It's not like that in Alsace," M Stoeckel said decisively. "French *choucroute* has quite a delicate taste, not at all overpowering, and needs a correspondingly delicate wine. The acidity and fullness of a Riesling will contrast splendidly with your rich duck meat and the gentle flavour of the *choucroute*."

The Wistub is, in its way, an epitome of Alsace, a room of sober colours, brown wainscoting and net curtains, comfortable on a raw day, filled with heat from a huge black- and green-tiled stove.

The clientele is unpretentious too: a few local bank staff having a birthday lunch, two businessmen, a courting couple. There is a sense of efficient bustle but never of too much haste as lunch, the focus of the day's activities, commences.

Outside, the Grand'Rue of Bergheim is hardly

▼ *The main street of Turckheim has the brightly-painted, wood-frame buildings with overhanging eaves so typical of Alsace.*

▲ *Jean-Marie Stoeckel – his food, typical of Alsace, combines French refinement with German vigour.*

◄ *The Wistub du Sommelier in Bergheim, a room of sober colours, brown wainscoting and net curtains.*

grand. It's simply a narrow street lined with half-timbered houses, often brightly painted, with overhanging eaves and highly ornate carving. These have somehow survived war, famine and modern development to give Bergheim an ancient, durable, solid and hard-working feel. And Bergheim is no exception to the rest of Alsace. While in so many regions of France village life and all its character is succumbing to the growth of large towns, or to the invasion of the impersonal, out-of-town superstore, here the local shops are lively, the activity palpable.

Every summer, a stream of cars and coaches crosses the Rhine from Germany, while many French come here to experience something slightly "foreign" without going abroad. The tourism is one reason why restaurants in Alsace are so abundant and of such good quality but, in winter, it is the keen local interest in Alsacien cuisine that keeps the shops and restaurants buoyant.

As if to test the worth of such strong local

▲ *Bernard Antony, Maître Fromager and enemy of processed cheese, displays the real thing.*

loyalty, I sampled the great cheese of Alsace: Munster. With Bernard Antony, a Maître Fromager – one of the heroes of French cheese – I tested supermarket Munster against the genuine article, farmhouse-produced – *le vrai* Munster (the true Munster) as Maître Antony called it. Inevitably, the difference was enormous between the smooth, tangy cheese made with unpasteurized milk, creamy at the edge, slightly chalky in the centre, and the mass-produced variety made with "dead" pasteurized milk, harsh and bitter. The best farmhouse Munster is ready from November to May (making it a winter cheese), since it takes four to five months from the time the cow grazes the summer pastures of the Vosges to our eating a slice of mature cheese.

The perfect partner for Munster is Alsace's Gewurztraminer wine, but I tried a slight variation – a Vendange Tardive, or "late harvest" Gewurztraminer, whose added richness and slightly sweet taste bore up the equally luxurious cheese.

I had started my visit to the region with another pairing, at the sort of evening an Alsacien loves. A hundred or so local restaurateurs had come together on their collective night off, but far from wanting the Alsace equivalent of baked beans on toast and early to bed, they were anticipating a substantial meal, plenty of wine and a very loud oompah band to dance to; and indeed the standard of dancing would have put to shame any local palais in a provincial British town.

At around midnight, when everybody else was just tucking into their main course, my hosts and I abandoned the proceedings. But we had started with what any food lover comes to Alsace for: *foie gras de Strasbourg*, superbly rich, smooth as chocolate, spicy, laced with alcohol – a magnificent speciality of the region, rivalling that from Périgord, in the southwest, for the title of finest in France. And what do you drink with this? In Bordeaux, they know the answer for their local *foie gras*: Sauternes. Here, the wine we are served is, unexpectedly for me, an excellent choice, because it is neither very sweet, nor is there an overplus of that acidity which is usually so important a factor in counteracting the richness of the *foie gras*.

My hosts, Olivier and Margaret Humbrecht, had been asked to provide a wine, and they suggested their own Domaine Zind-Humbrecht Pinot Gris Vendange Tardive – spicy wine, peppery, not highly acid, but with surprising elegance for such a gorgeous taste. This wine balances richness with refinement, echoing the similar qualities of the

▼ *The pastures of the Vosges Mountains at Col du Wettstein, and the cows that produce milk for Munster.*

► *Rich Alsace charcuterie in a shop in Colmar: the heart of Alsace food.*

foie gras, rather than acting as a foil to them.

The source of this *foie gras* was one of the many local charcuteries. Every village in Alsace, however small, has its own where, unusually for France, the charcutier combines his job with that of butcher. Pork is fundamental to the Alsacien diet – and the people have been masters in the art of its preparation since local Benedictine monks first became skilled in pig breeding.

M Sigmann's charcuterie shop, based in Ingersheim, just west of Colmar, is famous throughout Alsace. In his kitchens an army of charcutiers is making sausages, saveloys and black puddings, smoking hams, baking tarts and, of course, preparing fresh *foie gras*, which sits in state in neat pressed moulds, rather like gold bars – in price as well as appearance. These operations are not a sight for the squeamish, and certainly not one for the vegetarian (an idea that hardly occurs to the French), with huge mixers continually being filled

▲ *The tradition of fish eating in this land-locked region stems from the proximity of the Rhine.*

with highly individual assortments of meat, destined to fill metre-long strings of sausage.

Many people dislike the idea of geese or ducks being methodically fattened to enlarge the liver artificially – the only excuse I can plead is the sublime taste of *foie gras*. But, for M Sigmann, these moulds hold one of the greatest culinary sensations: whole livers, lightly salted and with a dash of Port, pressed and chilled. They will emerge slightly pink inside, with delicate marbling, perhaps laced with black truffles from Périgord. Served with toast, they are, for most Alsaciens, simply what life is all about.

From such sublime heights, the sausage seems fairly humble – but there's more to it here than you might imagine. I found *saucisse de Strasbourg*, made with pork and beef, laced with pepper, cumin seeds and coriander, *saucisse de Montbéliard*, a pure pork sausage, *wienerlé*, pork and veal held together with lard, *saucisse noir*, and a black pudding made with blood, onions, bread, milk and vegetables, and moreover the delicate *saucisse de Lyon* (a town in Alsace, not the city in southern France), pork laced with truffles, an exotic and rare luxury, and even – and this shows the central European character of Alsace again – sausage with paprika.

A sweet, tantalizing smell of wood creeps from the huge ovens, where hams and sausages hang surrounded by smoke curling languidly upwards from deep layers of ash – the hams cured for three or four days, the sausages for just a few hours. The smoke lends an unmistakable, bittersweet taste to the meat – which, as everyone would agree on tasting, is so lean and succulent.

Out in the shop, there were terrines and the ubiquitous *presskopf* – literally "pressed head" – ham in jelly, layered with chopped parsley, known in Burgundy as *jambon persillé*. *Presskopf* is in every charcutier's window, usually in the shape of the bowl from which it has just been inverted, glistening and glowing, ready to be downed with a glass of Gewurztraminer, rich and tasting of lychees.

Then it was on to visit the shops of Colmar with Jean-Philippe Guggenbühl, chef at La Taverne Alsacienne, opposite M Sigmann's premises. The town is both the capital of the Haut-Rhin département and of the Alsace wine region.

The centre has been restored, but large areas of ancient housing in this medieval town remain intact. Other parts are laced with canals and quiet waterways, reminiscent of Amsterdam. The main shopping street, pedestrianized, is lined with windows displaying chic clothes and – surely acting as a barrier to ever wearing such items – tempting pastry shops. Even on a quiet Wednesday afternoon these are jammed full of matrons eating the most outrageous cakes and drinking hot chocolate, for all the world as if they were in Vienna rather than provincial France.

In the quarter known as Petite Venise (Little Venice), the Quai de la Poissonnerie, lined with fish shops, runs alongside one of the canals.

Talking of fish seems strange so far from the sea, but the River Ill, running through Colmar, at one time overflowed with carp, trout, pike-perch and – in days of purer water – crayfish. Then, curiously, there's a local taste for herring, which began when barrels of wine ferried up the Rhine to Holland were returned filled instead with these silvery fish. Herring are still sometimes called here by their Dutch name: *matjes*. Even more curious, you can buy kippers, called *bückling*, the German word for bloater.

Today, as in any other of the world's major cities, Colmar's shops have produce from all over the world, at all times of the year, and the idea of seasonality has all but disappeared. But it does linger on for certain vegetables: locally grown asparagus appears in the spring, dandelion leaves (*pissenlit*) in the summer, and, in the autumn, mushrooms of an infinite variety. And Alsace produces cabbage for *choucroute*, potatoes for *pflutters* (dumplings), onions for *zewelewai* and *flammekueche* (see recipes), radishes and an abundance of salad greens, all in the fertile plain leading down to the River Rhine.

The asparagus season begins in April, when these tender tubes have pride of place in the market. This is thick, white asparagus, not the thin green variety – described dismissively in Alsace as only suitable for soup. The vegetable is treated with an almost religious fervour here – there's a Confrérie des Asperges, and an annual Fête des Asperges held in the villages.

The asparagus grows in sandy soil near the Rhine, often on land which can support little else,

▼ *The Quai de la Poissonnerie in the centre of Colmar: a touch of Venice in Alsace.*

Tarte Flambée or Flammekueche

BACON, CREAM AND ONION PIZZA

This is an Alsacien pizza, cooked in a very hot oven and usually eaten with salad as a light summer meal. As with any pizza, the topping is your choice, but this version is traditional to Alsace, the recipe coming from Jean-Philippe Guggenbühl, chef of La Taverne Alsacienne in Ingersheim. Several smaller pizzas can be made, if preferred. To drink: a young Edelzwicker or Sylvaner.

Serves: 6 people

Preparation time: 30 minutes (plus 2¾ hours rising time)

Cooking time: 15 minutes

500g (1lb 2oz) *pain au pavot* (poppy-seed bread) dough (see below for ingredients and method)

15cl (5fl oz) *crème fraîche*

15cl (5fl oz) Fromage Blanc

2 generous tbsp olive or vegetable oil

2 onions, cut into thin rings

200g (7oz) smoked streaky or fatty bacon, cut into small circular slices

salt, pepper

For the dough

300g (10oz) plain white flour

100g (4oz) wholegrain flour

100g (4oz) rye flour

2 tbsp salt

1 tsp poppy seeds

15g (½oz) fresh baker's yeast

50g (2oz) butter

30cl (10fl oz) milk

Place the flour, salt and poppy seeds in a large mixing bowl. In a separate bowl mix together the yeast and butter to make a paste. Stir sufficient milk into the flour to give a smooth, thick, creamy consistency. Make a well in the centre and add the yeast mixture, then knead the dough until it is well-mixed and elastic. Leave in a warm place for about 2 hours until it has doubled in volume. The dough is best used as soon as it has risen.

Spread the dough out on a baking tray (the base of a cake tin can also be used) and leave the dough for 30–45 minutes to rise a little more.

Meanwhile, preheat the oven to 250°C (500°F, gas mark 9), or to its maximum temperature.

Mix together the *crème fraîche*, Fromage Blanc and olive oil. Season with salt and pepper. Spread the mixture on the dough and cover evenly with the onion rings and slices of bacon.

Place in the oven and cook for up to 15 minutes until the onions are golden and the edge of the bread is crisp but not too dry.

Cut into slices and serve at once.

and its short season coincides with the reopening of many local restaurants after the winter break. For a few weeks very little else is served.

Bunches are placed upright in boiling water so that the tips are just steamed, then transformed into mousse, quiche, salad or simply served with dollops of mayonnaise. And to drink? Asparagus is a difficult food to match, but Alsace provides the answer: a grapey, fruity, fresh Muscat wine.

If asparagus is worshipped only once a year, the temple of the pastry cook is open the whole year round. The Ferber family's pâtisserie stands in a small square in Niedermorschwihr, a village west of Colmar, tucked into the end of a valley away from the main wine route followed by tourists, but evidently more prosperous in earlier days to judge by its respectable stone-built merchants' houses decorated with coats of arms.

Christine Ferber is one of only 11 female Maître Pâtissiers in France. Her kitchen seems far bigger than is needed to satisfy local demand, until you learn that she supplies restaurants in Strasbourg and Colmar with her confectionery and pastries, as well as baking bread daily and making fresh chocolates. For her, traditional cake-making – such as the fish-shaped *poissons d'Avril* made for the first of April – is not only important in keeping alive and celebrating age-old festivals but also, as she says: "To avoid competing with the encroaching supermarkets, I must make products with a difference."

▼ *Preserving a tradition: Christine Ferber's jams hold the flavour of Alsace's orchards and hedgerows.*

Her range of home-made jams is a good example. There is an overwhelming choice of fruits in every conceivable combination: fruits of the hedgerow – bilberries, wild strawberries, wild apples, eglantines (sweet-briar); cultivated fruits – plums, peaches, morello cherries; even a jelly with white Muscat grapes held in suspension – a true labour of love since every grape must have its stalk and pips removed individually.

The jams are in the same tradition as the *eaux-de-vie* of Alsace, the fruit liqueurs. The Alsacien can distil almost anything, and will if given a decent crop – a practice which puts Alsace firmly in the same orbit as Switzerland and the Black Forest of Germany. In many homes and restaurants stands a line of tall, thin, white bottles in which lurk fearsomely-strong, powerful liquids – but tasted they seem to encapsulate the very essence of each fruit. They are conventionally drunk at the end of a meal, with pastries, but to a true Alsacien most times are suitable for a glass of something fiery, fruity and warming: it is the veritable *trou alsacien*, just as a glass of Calvados is the *trou normand* – the term for a glass of spirits drunk between courses to aid the digestion and urge on the appetite. Beyond this, *eau-de-vie* is used in cooking: in terrines, in rich meat dishes, in cakes and in fruit salads.

At one time, an ambulatory still would have travelled from farm to farm, distilling seasonal fruit for the farmer or wine producer. Few exist now, and only a handful of wine producers carry out their own distillation, making *marc* from dried grape skins. Increasingly, as the stills are more and more heavily taxed, and the hygiene regulations imposed by Brussels become more rigorous, it is the large-scale distillers who maintain what was once a simple, homespun tradition.

Small glasses of *marc de Gewurztraminer* were sending out rich wafts of perfume at the end of my leisurely lunch with Mme Faller – *châtelaine* of the Clos des Capucins, on the edge of the fortified town of Kaysersberg. As its name suggests, the Clos was once home to a monastery, and the kitchen, with its huge range, was evidently built for an era of meals on a gargantuan scale, to supply such numbers.

The Faller wines are widely seen as being among Alsace's top estate wines, and, as we tasted a selection of them before lunch, Mme Faller listed the

▲ *Ingredients ready for a* kugelhopf *and the finished article; Christine Ferber likes to decorate hers with almonds.*

▲ *The steep-pitched roofs of the village of Kaysersberg - expansion has to be upwards when the streets are so narrow.*

Kugelhopf

This deliciously light, almond-flavoured cake, with its distinctive high-sided, ridged shape and hollowed-out centre, is a classic dish in both Alsace and Germany. In Alsace it is often served filled with fruit or ice cream, but it can be just as delicious eaten plain in the morning at coffee time, or served with a rich Vendange Tardive wine made from Riesling or Pinot Gris. Every Alsacien household will have its own version of kugelhopf *– perhaps adding raisins or almonds. This is the basic recipe and it comes from Christine Ferber, Maître Pâtissier in Niedermorschwihr. You will need a large (1½ litre/6 pint)* kugelhopf *mould, available from good kitchen equipment shops.*

Serves: 6 people

Preparation time: 30 minutes (plus 4 hours rising time)

Cooking time: 45 minutes

500g (1lb 2oz) plain flour

5 tbsp caster sugar

15g (½oz) fresh baker's yeast

1 tsp salt

150 grams (5 oz) unsalted butter

20cl (7fl oz) milk

2 eggs (size 2)

vanilla or almond essence

eau-de-vie (optional)

icing sugar

Put the flour, sugar, yeast and salt in a large mixing bowl and then work in the butter by hand. Warm the milk. Beat the eggs lightly with the milk and then pour over the flour and butter mixture.

Add a few drops of vanilla or almond essence to taste and, if desired, a tablespoon of *eau-de-vie*. Mix vigorously with a spatula, or using a dough hook on an electric mixer, until the dough is supple and leaves the sides of the bowl, adding a little more flour if necessary, to achieve the right consistency. Leave the dough in a warm place for about 2 hours, to double in volume.

Butter the *kugelhopf* mould and push the dough into it, making sure the dough reaches the bottom and fills all the ridges. Cover with a cloth and leave for about 2 hours until it has doubled in volume again.

Preheat the oven to 200°C (400°F, gas mark 6). Place the mould in the oven and cook for 45 minutes or until the *kugelhopf* is golden and starts to come away from the edge of the mould. Remove the cake from the mould while still warm and leave to cool on a wire cooling tray.

Sprinkle with icing sugar just before serving.

▲ *Mme Colette Faller and her daughter Catherine: exponents of the value of matching Alsacien food and wine.*

dishes she felt complemented each grape variety – some of which we would soon be sampling. Muscat, as we have seen, with asparagus, and as an apéritif; crisp, light Sylvaner with oysters, spicy sausages or *presskopf*; Pinot Blanc, fat and concentrated, with *tarte à l'oignon*, *quiche lorraine*, or mushroom dishes.

We reached Riesling. There was a pause of reverence for what many wine producers in Alsace regard as the finest grape variety. "Riesling", said Mme Faller, "is for fish, and, of course, to accompany classic Alsacien recipes: *coq au Riesling* (chicken in Riesling sauce), or *sandre au Riesling* (sander in Riesling)." Then there was another pause as Mme Faller disappeared to find a bottle of Pinot Gris (until recently also sold as Tokay d'Alsace): "This", she proclaimed as she returned, "can be drunk with roast veal, roast chicken and even lamb, with duck, turkey and spicy meats." It's the Alsacien equivalent of other regions' red wines – of which Alsace only produces a very small quantity from the Pinot Noir. And then there's Gewurztraminer, the richest of all Alsace wines and Munster's best partner.

Vegetable soup was the only course at lunch without a wine, but I took a sip of some Sylvaner I had in my glass and found it worked well. Onion tart was, as promised, a match for the Pinot Blanc, the wine's full flavour and slight acidity contrasting with the rich sweetness of the pastry and onions.

Lentils with beef balls, flavoured with onions

► *The country kitchen at Clos des Capucins, home of the Fallers, laden with Alsace dishes. The region's classic onion tart is at the front and, behind, are sausages and* choucroute, kugelhopf, *Munster cheese, smoked ham, meat terrine with gherkins, and local trout.*

Tarte à l'Oignon or Zewelewai

ONION TART

One of the classic flans of Alsace, for which everybody has their own personal recipe. This version comes from Christian Zimmerlin, whom I met on my travels, chef and patron of the Auberge de Brand in Turckheim, which lies in the shadow of the grand cru *Brand vineyard. A Riesling or Sylvaner is a good partner, having enough acidity to balance the sweetness of the onions.*

Serves: 8 people

Preparation time: 45 minutes (plus 2 hours resting time)
Cooking time: 20–25 minutes
400g (14oz) *pâte brisée*
(see below for ingredients and method)
1kg (2lb 4oz) onions
70g (2½oz) lean bacon
50g (2oz) butter, preferably unsalted
5 eggs (size 2)
50cl (17fl oz) single cream
salt, pepper

For the pâte brisée

25g (1oz) caster sugar
10g (½oz) salt, approximately
20cl (7fl oz) water
200g (7oz) unsalted butter
400g (14oz) plain flour

To make the pâte brisée

Dissolve the sugar and salt in the water. Cut the butter into small cubes and place in a bowl with the flour. Mix together by hand, but do not fully integrate the butter. Add the water slowly, blending all the time, until the mixture is smooth enough to come away from the edge of the bowl easily, but do not overwork. Add a little more flour or water if the pastry is either too soft or too stiff.

Cover the pastry lightly in flour and leave to rest in the fridge for a couple of hours. (The pastry will keep for 2–3 days in the fridge.) Roll out the pastry into a circle about 3mm(⅛in) thick and line an 8in flan case.

To make the filling

Preheat the oven to 200°C (400°F, gas mark 6). Chop the onions into fine strips and dice the bacon. Heat the butter in a frying pan and sweat the onions and bacon until the onions have lost most of their moisture, but have not browned. Put the pan on one side to cool.

Beat the eggs and cream, seasoned with salt and pepper, until light and frothy. Add the mixture to the pan containing the onions and bacon. Stir together until thoroughly blended and then pour into the flan case. Place in the oven and cook for 20–25 minutes.

The flan is best served very hot, but can also be eaten cold. A crisp green salad is excellent with this creamy flan.

and a bay-leaf, followed: true farmhouse cooking, hearty food for famished vineyard workers at harvest time. The lentils are soaked only briefly in water before being properly softened by the meat juices. This was a cue for a touch more Pinot Blanc, but for the next course Pinot Gris was produced:

▼ *Allow plenty of time to recover after eating a substantial* Baekeofa; *the pot is always brim-full.*

▲ *Mme Humbrecht reveals the results of long, slow cooking; her* Baekeofa *is one of the most authentic in Alsace.*

the rich wine was needed to march with sausages, a potato salad and gherkins. Finally, almost satiated, I was offered creamy Munster and Gewurztraminer.

That evening, presenting myself for dinner at the vineyard house of Olivier and Margaret Humbrecht, I wondered how I could survive for long in Alsace. "There's only one course," I was assured, as I sipped a glass of mineral water. "it's a *baekeofa*, a special Alsacien stew, which Olivier's granny has made."

As her recipe shows, this is not a dish to be entered into lightly. But such was the unbelievable richness of the flavours that came out of the flower-painted earthenware pot as the pastry strip was removed and the lid lifted, that, somehow, my appetite revived. This was a dish of superlatives, not just in size, but in character. The marinating of the meat, the slow cooking, the sealing in of all the tastes and aromas, created something quite extraordinary. And the full, spicy, concentrated taste of the Pinot Gris which we drank with it, seemed to make the eating all the easier.

Alsacien cuisine may not be food for the nobleman's table, I thought as I passed the last of the Alsace vineyards at their southern extremity at Thann (part of the Zind-Humbrecht domain) on leaving the region, yet it has the same qualities that are intrinsic to its wines – honesty, a concern for taste and comfort, and, above all, enjoyment. Not a bad combination at all.

Baekeofa or Baeckeoffe

PORK AND LAMB CASSEROLE

The name means "baker's oven" and, traditionally, the dish was served at lunch-time on washday. It was prepared the day before, taken in the morning to the local baker to be cooked slowly in his bread oven while the week's laundry was being cleaned, and then collected at lunch-time. It is still best prepared a day in advance and cooked slowly. To drink: a Pinot Gris.

Serves: 8–10 people

Preparation time: 1 hour (plus 12 hours marinating time)
Cooking time: 2½ hours
800g (1lb 12oz) shin of pork
800g (1lb 12oz) shoulder of lamb
2 pig's trotters
1 pig's tail
(Shin of beef can be added, or used as an alternative meat)
175g (6oz) pastry (made with flour, water and cooking oil)
3 large onions, thinly sliced
3 leeks, cut into 1cm/½in slices
2 kilos (4lb 7 oz) potatoes
1 bouquet garni
salt, pepper

For the marinade

1 garlic clove, crushed
1 onion, chopped
1 sprig thyme
1 bay-leaf
1 bottle white Alsace wine (Sylvaner or Pinot Blanc)
salt, pepper

Cut up the meat, including the pig's trotters and tail, into pieces about 4cm(1½in) sq. Prepare the marinade by putting the garlic, onion, thyme and bay-leaf together in a bowl with the wine. Put in the meat, season with salt and pepper and leave overnight in a cool place.

The following day, preheat the oven to 200°C (400°F, gas mark 6). Cut the potatoes into thin slices and sprinkle a little salt over them. Take the meat out of the marinade and put to one side.

In a large casserole dish (traditionally a big, deep earthenware pot) place a layer of potatoes, onions and leeks. Put in the meat and cover it with a second layer of vegetables. Pour over about a quarter of the marinade, add the bouquet garni and season with salt and pepper. Put the lid on the casserole dish and seal round the edge with the pastry, rolled into a long rope, to keep the flavour in.

Place the dish in the oven and cook for 2½ hours.

Serve directly from the casserole dish, breaking the pastry seal gently before opening. *Baekeofa* needs little more than a light salad as accompaniment; thick noodles – a favourite Alsacien garnish – could also be served, but this is approaching gluttony.

WINES OF ALSACE

The old saying is that the wines of Alsace are French wines made from German grape varieties; but while that epitomizes the chequered history of the province – periodically belonging to Germany, now a part of France – it only goes some of the way towards explaining what sets Alsace wines apart from those of the rest of France.

Alsace wines come from a long, narrow strip of vineyard lying on the eastern slopes of the Vosges Mountains in northeast France. The vines face across the River Rhine and towards the German vineyards of Baden. Curiously, despite the fact that they lie so far north, Alsace's vineyards are some of the driest and sunniest in the country, protected by the mountains from the wet weather moving in from the west. Often you will see dark storm clouds brooding above the Vosges while the vines bask in sunlight.

▲ *Large old barrels – traditional containers for wine in Alsace in the cellars of Kuentz-Bas in Husseren-les-Châteaux.*

One of the most crucial differences which sets Alsace wines apart is found in the simplest of forms – the label. Alsace wine bottles are the easiest in France to understand. The label, for once, tells you all you need to know about the contents. It gives standard pieces of information – the vintage, who made the wine – but it also reveals the one thing that so few French wines vouchsafe: the grape variety. In fact, Alsace is the only wine region in France where the grape variety is mentioned before the vineyard name.

Most Alsace wines are dry, despite the Germanic influence of some grape varieties, such as Riesling and Sylvaner. And, with one exception, all the wines are wholly based on one of seven grape types: six white, one red. The aim of Alsace wine producers is to enhance, to display to the full, the qualities of the grape variety, to reflect the grape's character in as pure a way as possible in the wine.

In other words, to emphasize the soft delicacy

► *Vineyards backed by the protective slopes of the Vosges Mountains surround Kaysersberg.*

of Pinot Blanc (also known locally as Klevner), the crisp, uncomplicated acidity of Sylvaner, the fresh grapey taste of Muscat, the elegance and zing of Riesling, the full, fat smoky flavour of Pinot Gris (until recently called Tokay d'Alsace), the opulent perfumed fruit of the Gewurztraminer. And, if they are making a red wine, they will try – with increasing success – to bring out the soft tannins and ripe fruit of the Pinot Noir.

The one exception is Edelzwicker, a wine made with a blend of different grapes (usually Sylvaner and Chasselas) and which, for most producers, is their basic table wine.

If Alsace wines are, on the whole, "single-minded" in terms of grape variety, they are "broad-minded" when it comes to being matched with food. They display a remarkable tolerance, happily partnering foods that are notoriously difficult to match. A Muscat, dry but highly scented, with hints of lavender, is one of the few wines that counters the inherent bitterness of asparagus and artichoke. A young, fresh Gewurztraminer is probably the only wine that can cope with the essential sweetness of Chinese cooking.

Although white wine is always the starting – and generally the finishing – point in any Alsace meal, the wines are carefully chosen to follow the weight and richness of what is certainly the most substantial cuisine in France. And, as you sip a Riesling while tackling a dish of lamb or venison – quite strong-tasting meats – it is gratifying to see how happily the white wines of Alsace replace the red

wine you would, in another region, have expected as accompaniment.

Another crucial difference between Alsace and the rest of France – and one which has contributed in no small measure to the reliable quality of the wines – is the rule that all Alsace wines have to be bottled in the area of production. As a result, no large négociants (merchants) from elsewhere in France have been able to buy up Alsace wine in bulk and ship it for bottling elsewhere; authenticity is therefore guaranteed. (The local négociants, who still dominate the trade, are comparatively small and deal only in Alsace wines.)

Until 1985, all Alsace wines were sold under the one appellation, Alsace appellation contrôlée, which made life simple for consumers, but did not enable them to distinguish between grapes from good vineyard sites and those from poorer areas. For this reason a superior appellation, Alsace Grand Cru, was created affording recognition to wines produced from some of the best, or "noble", grape varieties – Riesling, Gewurztraminer, Pinot Gris and Muscat – when grown in the finest of Alsace's vineyards. There are now 48 Grand Cru vineyards, and the name of each appears on the wine label alongside the words "Grand Cru".

Just to add a little spice to the story, wines made from the four "noble" grape varieties are not necessarily granted Grand Cru status even if they are the product of a single Grand Cru vineyard. One such vineyard may only be able to confer that honour on its Riesling wines, leaving any Gewurztraminer, Pinot Gris or Muscat to languish under the basic Alsace appellation. As yet another twist, a few vineyards which are not Grand Cru, but have a reputation for superb quality (including Clos Sainte-Hune of Trimbach and Herrenweg of Domaine Zind-Humbrecht) are also allowed to put their vineyard name on the wine label.

Two further categories of table wine exist in Alsace. These are rare and correspondingly expensive, but are the Alsacien equivalent of Sauternes or of German dessert wines. In good years, when the grapes reach the right level of ripeness, some bunches are left for late picking, to make a wine with a greater intensity of flavour known as Vendange Tardive – late harvest. Exceptionally, some bunches may develop the "noble rot", which shrivels the berries and gives a very high concentration of sugar. These bunches, or individual

▼ *The wine route proves popular for German visitors from across the Rhine as much as for the French.*

berries from them, are made into wines known as Sélection des Grains Nobles. Neither of these wines will be as overtly sweet or have the lusciousness of Sauternes or Trockenbeerenauslese: their character will be more powerful and unctuously rich, and they will always have an underlying predisposition to dryness – the hallmark of the region's wines. In Alsace, their place is almost as a separate course at the end of the meal, a moment in which to meditate on the quality of the wines you have drunk, before taking coffee and the inevitable (and heart-warming) *eau-de-vie*.

There is one further style of wine produced in Alsace: sparkling Crémant d'Alsace, often served as an apéritif. This is a bottle-fermented wine – whose production has increased in the last ten years – sometimes made with a blend of Chardonnay (which, in Alsace, can only be used for sparkling wine) and Pinot Noir, although Pinot Blanc and Pinot Auxerrois are more often used.

While vineyards can be found almost up to the German border in the north, the best areas start south of Strasbourg, centring on Sélestat in the north and Colmar in the south, with the finest wines generally agreed to come from the southern half of the region (the Haut-Rhin département). A series of wine villages, full of picturesque nooks and crannies and half-timbered houses, is dotted along a wine road that winds its leisurely way between vineyards which creep up the slopes of the Vosges on one side, and crawl down towards the River Rhine on the other.

The size of the vineyards here is tiny. There are 28,000 separate vineyard holdings, only 2,000 of which cover more than two hectares. This explains the dominance of the local négociants and cooperatives – who may buy in grapes and carry out the vinification themselves, or buy wine and undertake its *élevage* (maturing). Together they take the produce of nearly 84 per cent of the 9,000 or so individual growers. Only recently have growers who make and bottle their own wine made any great impression on the wine scene in Alsace: but it is surely significant that some of the very best wines in the region come from these grower/producers.

These top wines can age gracefully for many years. Indeed, one of the misconceptions about Alsace wines is that they should be drunk young because of the common belief that all white wines are better in their youth. Anyone who has had the chance to taste ten-year-old Riesling or Pinot Gris, or a venerable Gewurztraminer will know that age brings out complexities and character that the young wine will almost certainly lack. Any Alsace wine needs two, or preferably three, years before being drunk; for a Grand Cru, five or six years is a more realistic time-span.

▲ *Vines trained on wires held with concrete stakes are still a rare sight in Alsace; these are above Riquewihr.*

Perhaps it is because Alsace wines are drunk too young that they are still so under-appreciated outside France. Perhaps it is the confusion between Germanic grape varieties and a "French" taste – similar to the region's food, in fact, which may be German in name, but is quite French in nature. And yet I still cannot understand why the world does not drink more Alsace wines. They taste good, they are reliable, but, above all, in today's world, where white wines are in huge demand and short supply, here is a range that makes the great leap from apéritif to food wine with effortless ease, and gives great pleasure.

ALSACE

OTHER SPECIALITIES OF THE REGION AND WINES TO TRY WITH THEM

▲ *The beginning of the asparagus season in April is eagerly awaited.*

Alsace food, in its combination of German ingredients and French elegance, is a reflection of the region's wines. Expect to eat well – and solidly – here from a range of restaurants that makes Alsace one of France's premier gastronomic areas.

The variety of sausages made in Alsace is immense. There's **blutwurshet**, a black pudding made with pigs' blood, onions and spices, often prepared to secret recipes, and **schwarzwurshet**, a black sausage which usually comes smoked. **Knacks de Strasbourg** are sausages of veal or pork, very spicy and best grilled; **landjaeger** – also known as **gendarmes** – are beef or pork sausages which are cooked and then sliced into soup. **Schieffala**, smoked or salted shoulder of ham, appears as a garnish to **choucroute** (shredded, pickled cabbage) or is served in a more potent combination, with **sauce raifort** (horseradish sauce).

To drink: *a spicy wine such as a Gewurztraminer.*

Pike, tench, carp and eel lifted from the River Ill, which flows through Alsace's vineyards, are gathered together into a stew known as **matelote de l'Ill**. The fish are cooked whole (without the heads) with eggs, cream and Riesling.

To drink: *the Riesling used as an ingredient – preferably a crisp, full one.*

Strasbourg's cuisine reveals a strong Jewish influence, but the traditional Jewish recipes have often been given a French touch with the addition of local ingredients and wine. For **Carpe à la juive**, a dish usually served cold, the fish is braised in white wine with shallots, onions and herbs.

To drink: *as Alsace's driest and most acidic wine, Riesling is ideal with fish.*

Similar to the English Melton Mowbray pie is **Munster pie**, made with pork, onions and spices and eaten cold.

To drink: *an aromatic wine such as a Muscat.*

Riesling frequently appears as an ingredient, perhaps because it is the least aromatic of Alsace's wines. There is **coq au Riesling**, chicken in a wine and cream sauce, or **tourte vosgienne**, a puff-pastry pie filled with shallots, parsley, marinated pork and Riesling, and held together with Fromage Blanc. The *tourte* can be eaten hot or cold.

To drink: *Riesling would, again, be the best partner. Being elegant and not overpowering, it is the best all round food wine in Alsace.*

Spätzle, or noodle dumplings, accompany Alsacien dishes where, further south, pasta or rice would be served (reflecting either the Spanish or the Italian influence on French cooking). These small noodles made of semolina and flour are a favourite with game dishes such as **faisan à la vosgienne**, a pheasant, noodle and mushroom pie. **Noques** and **pflutters** are variations on the dumpling theme: *noques* are sometimes served with

▲ *The priorities of Alsace food – bread, wine and charcuterie.*

soup, while *pflutters* are tasty on their own, simply with a dab of butter.

To drink: *a Pinot Gris or Pinot Noir has the weight and richness to balance game dishes.*

Oie à l'alsacienne, roast goose stuffed with *choucroute* and sausage, (and often accompanied with *spätzle*) is a delicious dish for winter celebrations. In the autumn there is **cuissot de chevreuil aux poires**, haunch of venison with pears.

To drink: *again, heavier meats require a richer wine, such as a Pinot Gris.*

After a hard day's work tending vines or walking in the Vosges, a good Alsacien appetite-satisfier is **schieffala**, shoulder of salted pork, served with a mixture of mashed potato and finely chopped onion, with lashings of mustard and a green salad on the side.

To drink: *a Pinot Gris, rich and spicy.*

Before a meal, crisp **pretzels** may be served. Shaped like an open knot, these bone-dry biscuits, topped with a thirst-inducing sprinkle of coarse salt, are a common partner for beer.

Cherry soup, **soupe aux cerises**, is traditionally eaten on Christmas Eve. The cherries are cooked in red wine and the liquid is then poured over slices of fried bread.

To drink: *a wine with acidity and freshness, such as a Sylvaner.*

The vast array of hedgerow and orchard fruits in Alsace and the Vosges Mountains translates itself into a succession of fruit tarts – local pastry shops sell magnificent examples. The tarts are usually open and on shortcrust pastry; a particular speciality of Alsace is the **tarte aux myrtilles**, made with bilberries.

To drink: *Alsaciens might choose a Vendange Tardive with these desserts, but they would be just as likely to pause here before moving on to savour one of the enormous array of* eaux-de-vie *(fruit brandies), for which Alsace is famous.*

Eaux-de-vie are also used locally in cooking: in terrines, where their flavour can lift the weight of heavy ingredients, or in desserts such as sorbets, which may be made entirely of *eau-de-vie* (*eau-de-vie de Gewurztraminer* sorbet is particularly good), or with fruit and *eau-de-vie*. Kirsch (from cherries), Poire Williams (from pears), and Mirabelle (from plums) are the most famous of these drinks.

BORDEAUX

AND THE SOUTHWEST

In the jumble of narrow streets that forms the old quarter of Bordeaux the sedate medieval church of Saint-Pierre stands marooned in the empty pedestrianized square. At half past five in the morning, apart from an occasional passing cat and the rattling of our van echoing off the buildings, all is quiet.

But as M Barbier points his vehicle up one of the alleys leading out of the square the early morning calm changes. At the end of the alley, a sizzling array of lights suggests a gallery of all-night cinemas. The traffic suddenly doubles, trebles and multiplies, weaving around parked vans sticking out at awkward angles. And then we burst onto a scene of indescribable chaos.

The morning market at the Marché des Capucins is in full swing. Vans and tiny cars block the streets as they are loaded to the gunwales with fruit and vegetables, whole carcasses of meat, slabs of fish, and wriggling eels. Shouts issue back and forth as yet more van drivers stream in from every direction. Market porters wheel trolleys with total disregard for human life. There is a chorus of roars from stallholders in the interior of the concrete building, whose structure is all but obscured by produce hanging from every corner and pillar.

We join the dance of cars circling the building, looking to park. A ruthless jettisoning of some packing cases unblocks a space and M Barbier then charges out of the van, releases his young chef from the back, and we set out patrol-style for the day's shopping.

Jean-Paul Barbier is chef-owner of the Lion d'Or restaurant in Arcins, a small village in the heart of the Médoc vineyards, to the northwest of Bordeaux. He visits the Marché des Capucins three times a week, starting out at the unconscionable hour of five in the morning.

Well before reaching the meat stalls, M Barbier announces his presence simply by shouting at the top of his voice. At first, it appears that nobody has

▼ *The Lion d'Or restaurant in Arcins; bring your own wine to accompany Jean-Paul Barbier's superlative food.*

taken a bit of notice. But then from one corner a pile of boxes staggers forwards, and a small man is revealed beneath. This is part of a meat order made the day before. "I always deal with the same people, so that I can trust them," says M Barbier, "but I like to make sure I'm right in trusting them" – with which he peers with an expert eye into boxes and trays filled with steaks, ducks and trussed chickens.

Leaving his chef to take the boxes out to the van M Barbier presses on to the next stand. With a few more shouts, three whole lambs are displayed and, after a few clutchings of wrists – hands are normally too greasy at meat stalls to be grasped and shaken – these too are purchased. The season for this milk-fed lamb is very short: from Easter until the end of May or early June. *Agneau de lait de Pauillac* is so highly regarded that it has been given its own appellation contrôlée. The lamb derives its particular, intense and slightly salty flavour from its diet of milk, since the ewes graze the marsh areas of the Médoc where the grass is heavily impregnated with sea salt (the Gironde is tidal at least as far as the port of Pauillac, capital of the Médoc). At the Lion d'Or large cuts of this succulent meat are served lightly dressed with rosemary or other simple herb garnish and generally consumed with fine Bordeaux brought by M Barbier's wine-producing customers – the restaurant partly owes its local popularity to the fact that you can bring your own wine.

Then, it's rapidly on to fish. Here, as often as not, the product is still alive. We buy a crate of squirming lampreys – long, ugly, black eels – a huge, 70-kilo shad, shiny and fat, in all probability caught just a few hours earlier in the Gironde, the wide estuary formed where the rivers Garonne and Dordogne join, which runs north of Bordeaux out to the Atlantic. With these purchases, M Barbier has the two great fish delicacies of Bordeaux.

And so it goes on. By this time vegetables have also been piled into the van: fruit from the broad, fertile Garonne Valley – the area is famous for its succulent prunes from Agen, which sometimes come steeped in Armagnac and appear in both meat dishes and desserts – alongside white asparagus and lettuce from the wider Gironde region, with shallots and garlic – essentials of Bordelais flavouring.

Finally, across the square, we visit the aristocratic premises of a *foie gras* purveyor, a sudden oasis of calm and a place for silent worship and contemplation while the shop assistants fetch six livers from the cool room; at 216 francs a kilo, the shop can afford to be rather smart.

▲ Foie gras *and sweet Barsac – classic partners in a region where sweet wine is also drunk as an apéritif.*

The van is now so full that the poor chef has to crouch among the colourful crates and squirming livestock as we groan our way towards the cash and carry on the edge of the city, where M Barbier buys trout and salmon ("it's better here" he says – whoever said that of the British cash and carry?).

By eight o'clock, running a little late, we are back on the D2 to Arcins – the main route through the Médoc vineyards – going against the commuter traffic heading into Bordeaux.

The Médoc is a flat stretch of land, some 130 kilometres long, running up to the ocean on the left bank of the Gironde. The landscape may be featureless, the villages often little more than hamlets, but it is home to some of the world's most valuable vineyards, to the great châteaux of Margaux, of Saint-Julien, of Pauillac and of Saint-Estèphe. The gravel soil of the southern part, or Haut-Médoc, has the top quality vineyards – with outcrops of this soil also producing particularly good wines to the north.

The Bordeaux wine region straddles the Gironde estuary, extending south in a wide embrace to encircle land around the rivers Garonne and Dordogne. Overlooking the Gironde is the lovely, pale pink Château Loudenne, about ten miles from Lesparre, a busy market town acting as a centre for the northern Médoc. It was from a comfortable bed here that I had wrenched myself to make the dawn visit to the market in Bordeaux. The château,

▼ *Château Loudenne at Saint-Yzans-de-Médoc; two flags indicate the dual loyalty of this British-owned château.*

► *Vineyard at Château Mouton-Rothschild; the thick layer of stones visible in the soil is a sign that this is high quality land for vine-growing.*

▲ *The Lake of Lacanau, separated from the Atlantic coast by a wide strip of pine-covered dunes.*

run by English Master of Wine Charles Eve, is not only a large wine estate, which welcomes visitors for tastings, but also home to a wine school which attracts enthusiasts from around the world.

Meals at Loudenne are prepared by one of the foremost château cooks in the region, Josette Riondato. A native of Lesparre, married to an Italian, Mme Riondato has been at the château for 26 years, and from her I learned much about the history of the region and its cuisine. It was she who told me, for instance, that the very reason for agricultural poverty in the Médoc is what makes it a superb producer of fine wines.

In the early 19th century, before vineyards were planted widely in the Médoc, sheep and a few goats were all the thin gravelly soils could sustain. Where there were vines, sheep were kept to provide fertilizer for the plants as well as meat and wool for the vinegrower. Vines now dominate the gravel plateaux, and positively thrive in the same poor soil, while the sheep have been relegated to the low-lying areas between these gentle slopes, or to pastures along the Gironde estuary. A reminder of the pre-eminence of sheep in earlier times is found in the name of one of the region's most famous châteaux: Mouton-Rothschild – in the local dialect, *moutonnier* is the name for a shepherd.

For dinner that evening Mme Riondato was preparing *alose*, shad, as a first course – this one came from neighbouring Saint-Estèphe, formerly a busy port, now known for being the biggest wine commune of the Médoc. I had seen the fishermen's rickety cabins, hanging out over the water along the marshy banks of the estuary, held up by no more than a few rotting pieces of wood.

The shad is a big fish, long and with piercing, mournful eyes. The flesh is oily, rather like a sardine, and has a strong flavour. Mme Riondato slit open the body to reveal row upon row of tiny bones, just waiting to catch you in the throat. First, she washed the shad and scraped off the scales to reduce the saltiness of the skin then, very carefully, she filleted it and cut it into steaks. It was cooked that evening, over a fire of vine cuttings which filled the large open fireplace, and served with a light sauce of shallots – a lovely green against the dark flesh of the fish. Château Loudenne produces a delicious dry white Bordeaux. This is unusual for the Médoc, where most wine is red, but it was typical of Bordeaux as a whole in its blend of Sémillon and Sauvignon Blanc grapes – a combination which has enough weight and freshness to counterbalance the assertive flavour of the fish and to cut through its slightly oily texture.

Next came the famous *agneau de lait* (see recipes), simply roasted in a little olive oil and seasoned with garlic, rosemary, thyme and sage. The meat juices are deglazed with a little wine vinegar and thickened to give a rich sauce made piquant by the hint of vinegar. This combination of flavours is, for the English, similar to serving lamb with mint sauce, but whether the custom of adding vinegar to lamb was started by a visiting English milord, or borrowed from winemaking friends in Bordeaux remains a mystery.

The marriage of claret – the English term for red Bordeaux – and lamb is one made in heaven and hallowed by generations of English Sunday lunches. But when cooked in the Médoc, the lamb is, properly, pink when sliced – would that it were more often in England. This succulent meat was perfectly matched with a still youthful 1970 Château Loudenne, powerful and concentrated.

Faced with the cheese platter, I made a discovery: there are no cows' milk cheeses native to Bordeaux. In fact, Bordeaux is not a cheese-producing region, and the only local variety is a young, fresh, soft and creamy goats' milk cheese made by a farmer near Lesparre; the goat, being hardy, can survive better than the cow on the region's relatively poor pasture. The cheese, as other young goats' cheeses, goes well with young red wines – an appellation Bordeaux, or a Côtes de Bourg or Côtes de Blaye, which taste lighter, fruitier, and have less tannin.

The Bordelais have, however, created their own special version of a Dutch cows' milk cheese. The taste for Dutch cheese dates back as far as the 18th century, when it was traded for wine. Gouda was imported and then matured to a depth of flavour quite unheard of in Amsterdam's markets. It goes splendidly with older, mature reds – I tried a 1966 Château de Pez from Saint-Estèphe – reinforcing my feeling that, in comparison with this cheese, many of the stronger, runnier French cheeses can make unsuitable partners for red wine. An alternative and rather cheaper wine to try would be a young Graves from the 1980s.

For dessert, Mme Riondato had made a simple dish, one typical of Bordeaux: pears in red wine. The peeled fruit is simmered whole in sugar and

▼ *The trees of the Landes, Europe's largest pine forest, dominate for hundreds of kilometres south and west of Bordeaux.*

water, wine is poured in at the end of cooking and the liquid then reduced to a light syrup. The finished dish is served with *crème fraîche*. Local pears are used in season but, as Mme Riondato points out, "There's always plenty of red wine around."

A glass of Cognac, the local brandy of Bordeaux from Charente – the region to the northeast of the Gironde – to go with coffee in front of a log fire, rounds off what a very few would call a "simple" evening in a Bordeaux château, but which for most would linger in the memory for many, many years.

The following day I witnessed a somewhat macabre ceremony in preparation for the traditional dish *lamproie à la bordelaise* – lamprey cooked in red wine. In spring great numbers of this fearsomely ugly eel are caught in the waters of the Gironde. It is a complicated dish, taking two days to prepare. First, the lamprey must be bled. The live eel is hung by its head over a large bowl and allowed to bleed to death from cuts made in its tail. This is one of those activities which you have to accept as part of the normal process of food preparation in France, but it is still hard to watch. I must admit to being delighted to exit from the scene with Charles Eve. We were to drive into the countryside of Gascony, to the Landes, the largest area of pine forest in Europe, stretching down from Bordeaux, parallel to the Atlantic coast, south to Biarritz and the Pyrenees, and many miles inland.

The Landes is a place of compulsive repetition. For mile upon mile, straight empty roads plunge between dense ranks of trees, broken only occasionally by clearings where there may be market gardens or a small cluster of houses. Towns and even villages are few and far apart: this must surely be one of the emptiest parts of an often sparsely populated country.

In fact the forest of the Landes is artificial, the creation of a spectacular plan in the 19th century to stop the constant erosion of the sandy soil and coastal sand-dunes, buffeted regularly by the Atlantic storms which were threatening to engulf whole tracts of land.

In the heart of the Landes is the small town of Rion-des-Landes, which houses the restaurant of Maite Ordonez, one of the most well-known chefs in Gascony. Her televised cookery series, La Cuisine des Mousquetaires (after the Three Musketeers of Alexandre Dumas, one of whom,

Agneau de Lait de Pauillac

MILK-FED LAMB FROM PAUILLAC

The success of this recipe, as prepared by Josette Riondato at Château Loudenne in the Médoc, depends on the quality of the lamb. It should be true lamb, not mutton, and ideally the first of the season. The lamb is cooked very simply, with herbs and a little vinegar in the sauce, and should be accompanied by a good bottle of red Bordeaux, perhaps a Cru Bourgeois (wines in the second rank of Bordeaux's classification system).

Serves: 4–6 people
Preparation time: 15 minutes
Cooking time: 1 hour 5 minutes
1 leg of spring lamb, weighing about 1kg (about 2¼lb)
olive oil
thyme
sage
rosemary
1 onion, unpeeled
1 carrot
3 cloves garlic, unpeeled
15cl (5fl oz) chicken stock
1 tbsp wine vinegar (the amount depends on its strength; if sherry vinegar is used, less is needed)
salt, pepper

Preheat the oven to 200°C (400°F, gas mark 6). Put the lamb in a large roasting tin. Brush the meat with olive oil, season with salt and pepper, and sprinkle over the herbs.

Quarter the onion, slice the carrot and the garlic cloves, and add these to the tin.

Place the roasting tin in the oven and cook for about 45 minutes, so that the meat is brown on the outside, but still pink in the middle. While the lamb is cooking, heat the chicken stock. At the end of the cooking time, add the hot stock to the roasting tin and sprinkle the vinegar over the lamb. Return the tin to the oven and cook for a further 15 minutes.

Transfer the lamb to a warmed serving dish and cover with aluminium foil to keep hot. Drain the juices left in the roasting tin through a filter, pressing the vegetables hard. Degrease the juices by simmering them in a pan for about 5 minutes.

Pour the sauce around the meat, or place separately in a sauce-boat, and serve. Accompany with a selection of vegetables in season.

d'Artagnan, hailed from Gascony) has been a great success, focusing attention on the traditional cooking of the region.

Gascony is one of the great gastronomic regions of France, offering a richer cuisine, and having more natural resources, than the province of Guyenne, to the north. But this is richness tempered with rusticity: goose and duck, served in varying ways and in hearty quantities, are typical features of the region's cooking. The birds yield *foie gras* – firm-textured, rich livers – but their use goes beyond this luxury: goose fat is used in cooking in place of butter or oil, and surplus meat is made into terrines and *confits* – a good method of preserving and typical of the thrift of rural French cooks.

The Landes has an abundance of feathered game. Small songbirds, including, at one time, the thrush, have long been featured on Gascon menus. Now banned by law, hunting the thrush not only provided a delicate meat (often stuffed with *foie gras* or used in terrines), but also rid the vineyard of one of its worst pests at harvest time, when the birds stripped the vine of grapes before the vigneron could. Another wild bird, the ortolan, used to be caught and then fattened on grain and Armagnac, the brandy from Gascony, and the oldest in France. Cooking with Armagnac adds the final touch to this rural, and yet refined, cuisine.

Le Relais des Landes, Maite Ordonez's restaurant, is full and many customers seem to be locals. We are to sample the *foie gras* – the reason for our pilgrimage into the Landes – and not one but three different dishes arrive: *foie gras* flambéed with Armagnac – the dish is a local speciality – quite dry in taste and appearance, but with a good burnt caramel flavour; next *foie gras* with a peppercorn and cream sauce and, lastly, *foie gras* with sliced apples and port.

The Landes is the source of the finest Gascon *foie gras*. How, I wonder, does it differ from France's other famous variety, made in Alsace? "Strasbourg *foie gras* is treated as a terrine," I am

◄ *Geese and ducks – to the cooks of the Landes these represent the fine* foie gras *of Gascony.*

told, "it's marinated in wine and spices. In Gascony, *foie gras* is literally that – a duck or goose liver to which little is done apart from its being cooked, sliced and served." It is true that the art of making *foie gras* in Gascony seems to be to treat the raw material as little as possible. Refinements are only made just before it is served.

Charles Eve has brought three sweet white wines from Sauternes with him, to test the theory that *foie gras* is best accompanied by the luscious white wines of Sauternes and Barsac, and a few other appellations making *vins liquoreux* in the southern part of Bordeaux: Sainte-Croix-du-Mont, Loupiac, Cérons and around Cadillac in the Premières Côtes de Bordeaux. The question, however, is which style of sweet wine is best. So we have Château de Rayne-Vigneau 1986, a marvellous year, with the sweet taste but the dry finish characteristic of fine Sauternes, Château Filhot 1985, a more delicate and finely structured wine from a lighter year, and a 1990 Château Suduiraut, opulent

Salmis de Palombe

ROAST WOODPIGEON IN BRANDY AND RED WINE

"Salmis" *describes a dish in which game birds are partly roasted, then jointed and simmered in a wine sauce. Traditionally Gascon, the dish makes use of both red Bordeaux and Armagnac. Any small game bird is suitable, but success lies in using one well hung bird in the sauce. Drink a robust red Saint-Emilion or Médoc.*

Serves: 4 people

- Preparation time: 30 minutes
- Cooking time: 1½ hours
- 5 woodpigeons (one should be well hung, for the sauce)
- 70g (2½oz) butter, preferably unsalted
- 1 large onion, diced
- 30g (1oz) shallots, diced
- 2 large carrots, diced
- 1 garlic clove, finely chopped
- 2 tbsp plain flour
- 2 tbsp Armagnac (Cognac can be substituted)
- 50cl (17fl oz) chicken stock
- 1 tbsp tomato purée
- bouquet garni
- 50cl (17fl oz) red Bordeaux
- the game birds' livers, or 125g (4½oz) chicken livers
- salt, pepper

Remove the flesh from the woodpigeon for the sauce and cut into small cubes. Melt 20g (½oz) of butter in a frying pan, add the meat cubes, onions, shallots and carrots and cook on a medium heat for 8 minutes, stirring regularly. Add the garlic, then the flour, and stir for 4 minutes.

Pour 1 tablespoon of brandy over the pan and set alight. As the flames die, add the stock, tomato purée, bouquet garni and wine (keeping back 2 tablespoons of wine). Reduce the heat, cover and simmer for 1 hour.

Meanwhile, preheat the oven to 220°C (425°F, gas mark 7). When the sauce has simmered for 40 minutes put the other 4 woodpigeons into a greased roasting tin and roast in the oven for 20 minutes, until brown on the outside but still rare inside. Keep any juices in the tin.

When the sauce has simmered for 1 hour, adjust the seasoning and strain through a sieve. Return the liquid to the frying pan, and place over a moderate heat.

Drain the roasting tin of excess fat. Chop the livers finely, place in the roasting tin and cook over a low heat for 10 minutes. Add the second tablespoon of brandy and set alight. As the flames subside, add the rest of the wine and bring just to the boil, then keep warm.

Cut the birds in two with carving scissors, preserving any juices. Place them in the sauce in the frying pan, simmer for 5 minutes, then remove and put on a hot serving dish. Whisk the sauce, adding the livers and their sauce, any meat juices and the rest of the butter.

Pour the sauce over the woodpigeons and serve.

▲ *Jars of* pâté de foie gras. *The percentage figure on the label indicates the amount of pure* foie gras *awaiting you.*

► *Bottles of local wine from all over the Bordeaux region, gathered together for sale in Andernos.*

and intense. A Monbazillac from the Bergerac region in the Dordogne, to the east of Bordeaux, would be a less expensive substitute for these Sauternes wines.

Quickly the Filhot is ruled out as too light, unable to cope even with the relatively delicate *foie gras* and Armagnac. But the power of the two other wines works magnificently, the younger Suduiraut perhaps the better, simply because it is so concentrated. If there is a lesson here, it is that the extreme richness of *foie gras* can only be balanced by a rich, sweet wine. That the dish also works, curiously, with Bordeaux's own apéritif, Lillet, a sweet white vermouth (and a fraction of the price), is proof that the sweetness of the drink is the most important factor.

It's a lesson repeated with the cheese course, where we all choose Roquefort, the blue-veined cheese of the Landes. Made solely from ewes' milk and matured for a year until it is a soft yellow colour, it is at its best in spring and summer. It has a delicate flavour, not as strong as many blue cheeses, and, while the creamy, salty taste fails miserably with red wine (another reminder that red wine should never automatically be chosen with cheese), it seems almost to melt into the embrace of the Sauternes. The French rarely drink sweet wine with dessert (preferring champagne); instead they serve it as an apéritif or partner it with this sublime cheese.

But everyday Gascon food is every bit as good as the luxurious fare from the region. The bitter cold of the Pyrenees has provided the cuisine of southwest France with some robust broths and *pots-au-feu* for winter; cooked slowly overnight they, at one time, both nourished and warmed the family. *Garbure* from the Béarn region is typical of these, a thick garlic-flavoured soup, based on ham and duck (see recipes); and similar is the *sobronade* from Périgord, thick with pork, root vegetables, celery and haricot beans.

Hearty food this may be, but the cuisine of the far southwest has great finesse, is vibrant with colour and extrovert in flavour: hot peppers and tomatoes,

onions and garlic, cinnamon, cloves, saffron and herbs. Its essential ingredients show the influence of Spain and even further afield – maize was an early import from the New World, as were pumpkins which are a favourite soup. The Basque region is famous for its fish dishes: baby squid (*chipirones*), stuffed or casseroled, tuna with onions, and salt cod. But it was more northerly seafood that we were heading for as we left Rion-des-Landes for the oyster beds of Arcachon, also a resort town to the southwest of Bordeaux. The route leads through more swathes of pine forest, past small seaside towns to which the Bordelais flock during the school holidays for the miles of sandy beaches, the surfing and the sea-fresh oysters.

The Bassin d'Arcachon is an almost completely enclosed bay – a large, shallow, sea-water lake –

Garbure

GASCON BROTH

Soups have for long been a feature of the southwest's cuisine – cooked slowly in the cauldron which at one time hung over every hearth. This hearty meat and vegetable soup should sustain even the most ravenous, and at its best should be so thick that the ladle can stand up in the pot. This soup is excellent accompanied by a rich style of red Bordeaux – a Saint-Emilion would be very suitable, or a Fronsac or Côtes de Castillon.

Serves: 6–8 people
Preparation time: 15 minutes (plus 24 hours soaking time)
Cooking time: 3¼ hours
250g (9oz) dried kidney beans
knuckle of salted ham
500g (1lb 2oz) carrots, sliced
500g (1lb 2oz) turnips, sliced
700g (1½lb) leeks, sliced
1kg (2lb 4oz) potatoes, peeled and sliced
1 large cabbage, chopped roughly
half a duck, including the wing and leg
5 cloves garlic, chopped
duck fat (needs to be bought separately)

Soak the beans for 24 hours in cold water, changing the water every 8 hours.

Fill a large pan with cold water, add the ham and boil gently for 45 minutes. Drain the soaked kidney beans and rinse in fresh water. Add to the pan and simmer for 1 hour.

Add the vegetables to the pan, keeping back a quarter of the cabbage and 1 large sliced potato. Simmer slowly for 30 minutes.

Add the duck, including the leg and wing. Continue to simmer for a further hour, making sure the water does not boil.

A quarter of an hour before serving, blanch the remaining cabbage and sliced potato in a pan of boiling water for a few minutes. Add these to the soup.

Just before serving, thicken the whole by adding a good dash of duck fat to which the chopped garlic cloves have been added. To make it easier to eat, remove the ham-bone: the meat will be so tender that this should not be difficult.

calm and sheltered, in sharp contrast to the windy, bracing coast of the Bay of Biscay. At low tide, it seems more like a series of small rivulets than an inlet from the ocean, but this provides ideal territory for oyster beds. On its periphery are small, Proustian towns: Arès, Andernos-les-Bains, Arcachon itself, and, most chic of all, Cap Ferret.

In Andernos, a stroll around the peaceful bay brings me to a small hut in the middle of a grove of pines, close to the harbour: the headquarters of the local oyster fishers' association. Close by are the sheds of the fishermen themselves. And somewhere out there, in the midst of these expanses of salty mud lie the oyster beds, *les parcs à huîtres*, as they are marked on the Michelin map. The secret of outstanding quality in the oysters from Arcachon or Cap Ferret (both names are used) lies in the calm, warm water of the Bassin d'Arcachon, which has only a gentle salinity.

M Muyard, technical adviser to the oyster association, is keen to explain his subject before we taste, and there is much to learn – about the various sizes of oyster, for instance: the *huîtres fines* and the larger *huîtres spéciales*, classified by weight according to the proportion of flesh and liquid to shell (the more, the better, naturally), and a further type, the *claires*, which are *huîtres spéciales* matured

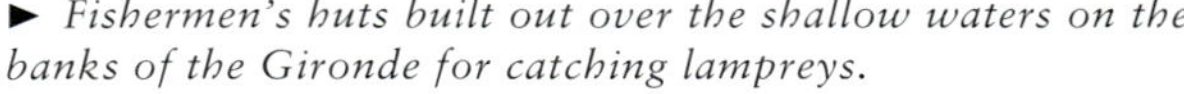

► *Fishermen's huts built out over the shallow waters on the banks of the Gironde for catching lampreys.*

◄ *Discarded oyster shells at Port de Goulée in the Médoc – somebody has a passion for them.*

further in saltwater tanks, and subject to more subdivisions according to size. Their taste comes from the type of plankton used in the tanks, which can vary, the overall effect of this farming being to give the oysters a finer flavour, one less obviously salty. The old size categories of *petite*, *moyenne*, *grosse*, and *très grosse*, M Muyard explained, are no longer legal, if still widely used.

At last, we are allowed to taste the Arcachon oysters. A dozen, arranged on paper plates, with slices of lemon and brown bread, give off the most delicious tang of the sea. Anxious to try these delicacies with local wines, I have brought three bottles: a young Sauvignon Blanc-based Entre-Deux-Mers (the white wine appellation for wines produced between the Dordogne and the Garonne rivers – the two "seas"), Château Loudenne Blanc, with a blend of Sauvignon Blanc and Sémillon – the same

Salade de Cresson avec Huîtres Tièdes

SALAD OF WATERCRESS AND WARM OYSTERS

Purists may say that the only way to eat oysters is fresh from the sea, with just a touch of lemon and plenty of brown bread, but this is an attractive alternative which preserves the ocean tanginess of the oysters, and makes a delicious light lunch with a glass of very dry white wine. I would suggest an Entre-Deux-Mers or a Bordeaux Sauvignon Blanc. The proportions here are for two people – allow six oysters per person. Instead of watercress, other salad leaves, such as rocket or endive, could be used.

Serves: 2 people

Preparation time: 20 minutes

Cooking time: 5 minutes

12 medium-sized oysters (*grosse*)

1 bunch watercress or other salad leaves

½ tbsp balsamic vinegar or sherry vinegar

1 tbsp olive oil

1 shallot, finely chopped

chives, chopped

parsley, chopped

freshly ground black pepper

Carefully open the oysters without damaging them. Remove the oysters from the shells, keeping them in the juice. Put aside in a saucepan with the juice.

Wash the watercress, discarding the stalks and any discoloured leaves.

Make a vinaigrette with the vinegar and olive oil, add the shallot, chives and parsley. Arrange the watercress or salad leaves in the centre of a serving plate and pour over the vinaigrette.

Bring the oysters quickly to the boil, reduce the heat and simmer for about 5 minutes, so that they become firm. Remove them from the pan and dry on absorbent paper.

Place the oysters, still warm, around the salad, and grind a little black pepper on top.

Serve and eat immediately.

one tried with the shad – and Château Carbonnieux 1985, from the Graves, upstream of Bordeaux, in its maturity tasting more of Sémillon than Sauvignon, with a heavier and more oily character. As the oysters slipped down effortlessly, it became clear that the higher acidity and green tastes of Sauvignon were able to cope by far the best with the sea-salty, tangy taste and that unique texture of oysters.

Returning to Château Loudenne that evening, I was able to sample the lamprey. The eel, cleaned, head removed and cut into medium-sized pieces, now looked more appetizing. Mme Riondato had added all the ingredients to a vast pot – onions, leeks, parsley and thyme, and a large quantity of red Bordeaux, mixed with the eel's blood to give an enormously rich sauce, only to be eaten in small quantities, but essential to sustain the strong gamey taste of the lamprey itself. Using wine to the full, it can be seen, is essential in Bordelais cuisine. With this dish a Château Pétrus 1964 made an exceptional combination, the wine so powerfully dense and concentrated – and yet still young – but a red Entre-Deux-Mers, or any wine with plenty of Merlot, which gives a softer, richer wine than those of the Médoc, would be a good alternative to try with this dish.

Local fish and game translated into a rich cuisine are the heart of Bordeaux and the southwest. Bordeaux is a land of great wines with a formidable international reputation – a reputation which, helped by the seaboard location, has made the region outward-looking and given it the prosperity to build imposing châteaux and encourage a taste for fine cuisine.

Yet this is a region where good agricultural land is rare and where vines, planted on the predominantly gravel-based soils, are often the only viable crop. In earlier days, food was often hunted rather than grown, imported rather than indigenous, and until the riches of wine appeared, many in the region must have lived a hand-to-mouth existence. It is only to the south and west that the land becomes more fertile and yields a richer cuisine – the luxuries of *foie gras* from Gascony and truffles

◄ *Sheep graze the low-lying pasture land of the Médoc, away from the higher ground, which is now devoted to cultivating vines.*

► *Spraying vines against mildew in Saint-Emilion, an essential task in the moist heat of the summer.*

◄ *The Gironde emptied to the low-water mark; just how much the water level varies in the estuary can be judged by the height of these platforms.*

from Périgord – but, despite this, the southwest's cuisine is neither extravagant nor ostentatious, having a strong tradition of practical, rural cooking.

It is perhaps ironic that the more barren land of Bordeaux has been the very cause of that region's productivity. Nowhere in France is the belief that great wines need poor land to flourish borne out so completely as in Bordeaux. It is here that this paradox has its fullest and greatest expression.

WINES OF BORDEAUX AND THE SOUTHWEST

It is no exaggeration to say that Bordeaux is the largest quality wine producing area in the world. The range of wines it produces is huge: from full-bodied dry whites balancing the herbaceous qualities of Sauvignon with the luscious fat fruit of Sémillon, to the finest sweet, white wines where the same grape varieties (infected with "noble rot", which concentrates the grape sugars) produce intense "honey and cream" wines. And, above all, is a range of superb reds: intellectual, elegant, ageing gracefully and splendidly. For many people, especially in Europe, red Bordeaux – claret as it is called in Britain – is the first red wine they encounter. Many stay with Bordeaux for the rest of their lives.

The vineyards of Bordeaux have a centuries-old link with Britain which dates back to the Middle Ages, when Gascony was ruled by the English kings and wines were shipped up the estuary of the Gironde, out to the Atlantic and so to Bristol and London. But these vineyards are at the heart of a much larger vineyard area in southwest France.

For much of their long history, the smaller wine-producing areas of the southwest have been overshadowed by their giant neighbour, whose seaboard location gave it a large measure of control over the wine market in this corner of France.

To the east of Bordeaux, in the Dordogne Valley, lies Bergerac, making wines that could easily pass for lighter versions of Bordeaux. The grape varieties are the same, but neither the heights nor the depths of Bordeaux are reached in Bergerac. To the south are the much smaller vineyards of the Côtes de Duras and Côtes du Marmandais. It is only because of a political decision stating that Bordeaux wines may only come from the Gironde département, that the wines from these three areas cannot be called Bordeaux. In taste, Duras and Marmandais wines, like Bergerac, are almost indistinguishable from basic Bordeaux.

Further afield is the ancient winemaking region of Cahors, its vineyards dating back to the time of the Roman occupation. The full-bodied reds for which it is famous can be very dense in colour – at one time these were known as the "black" wines of Cahors. Such wines need rich, sustaining food,

▼ *Château Ausone in Saint-Emilion. The rough track belies the high reputation and value of this château's wines.*

▲ *All over the Médoc, small vineyards offer a warm welcome to people who would like to taste or buy.*

since their tannins and "dusty" fruit can be quite overpowering when young, although the wines do soften with maturity. The region's links with the Bordeaux wine trade have, in recent years, relaxed, as the region becomes more independent.

Other wines of the southwest, further afield, have a more tenuous link with Bordeaux. The strange, evocatively-named grape varieties – Loin d'Oeil, Tannat, Fer – of Irouléguy, Jurançon, Madiran, Béarn and Tursan, set the Basque wines apart, while the wines of Gaillac and the Côtes du Frontonnais look as much to the Mediterranean as to the Atlantic in blending Bordeaux's grape varieties with those of the Midi: the Syrah and Cinsaut.

The strength of the southwest lies in the incredible variety of its wines: the curious, rather lean wines of Irouléguy, the fine, sweet wines of Jurançon, the bone-dry, peach-flavoured Pacherenc du Vic Bilh from Madiran. And each complements its local cuisine: the fruity, perfumed wines of the Côtes du Frontonnais partnering *cassoulet*, the substantial bean stew well-stocked with pork, mutton, duck or goose, also found in the Languedoc; the wines of Madiran, extremely tannic, accompanying the rich pork, duck or goose *confits* (conserves) and terrines of Gascony, and with the red-pepper flavoured dishes of the far southwest.

Many of these areas have contracted over the last century, but Bordeaux itself has grown in both size and influence. The major red grape varieties of Bordeaux – Cabernet Sauvignon, Cabernet Franc and Merlot – are now planted throughout the wine world: Merlot lending softness, roundness, richness; the Cabernet Sauvignon giving firm fruit and ageing ability, and Cabernet Franc offering pungency and spice.

On a smaller scale, the sweet, white dessert wines of Sauternes and Barsac (just to the south-east of Bordeaux), made from Sémillon and Sauvignon Blanc, and lesser appellations such as Sainte-Croix-du-Mont, Cadillac and Loupiac, have provided a model for similar wines produced as far apart as Australia and California.

In the Graves, the Sémillon and Sauvignon vines can benefit from long, warm autumns, with morning dew and afternoon sun, which together provide ideal conditions for "noble rot", allowing producers to make luscious long-lived wines with increasing confidence and success after some years of neglect in the world market and, consequently, in the standards of production. A great Sauternes balances this lusciousness against the dryness that is also a characteristic of "noble rot" wines, and which prevents them from being cloying.

But why should Bordeaux, more perhaps than any other wine region – even Burgundy – have influenced wine styles so much? It certainly has a great deal to do with the Cabernet Sauvignon, the principal grape variety of so many châteaux in the region. This amenable vine is happy to be transplanted to most continents and can adapt to most climates. But it also has much to do with Bordeaux's standing in the international wine trade – much helped by its position on the shores of the Atlantic. The region's traditional role of supplying claret to the British – often seen as the arbiters of wine taste – ensured that Bordeaux received enormous international recognition just at the time when the New World vineyards were starting up.

And there's no doubt that the status of Bordeaux has been enhanced by the fact that so much wine (as much as 600 million bottles a year) and so much excellent quality wine – comes out of this region. Terrifically good value can be found in cheaper red Bordeaux – under the basic Bordeaux appellation, or in Côtes de Bourg or Premières Côtes de Blaye – just as there are sublime experiences to be found in wines from the great estates.

Despite the number of different local names in Bordeaux, the region is organized simply and logically. To begin with, there is the great divide of the estuary and its two rivers. The Garonne and the Dordogne flow together just downstream from the city of Bordeaux to form the Gironde, the wide estuary which gives the administrative département its name. Despite having two rivers, Bordeaux's vineyards are still divided between right and left banks.

The term "right bank" is reserved for the northern bank of the Dordogne, which becomes the eastern bank of the Gironde as it flows almost due north into the ocean. "Left bank" refers to the southern bank of the Garonne and western bank of the Gironde. In between, the wedge-shaped piece of land between the two rivers is known as Entre-Deux-Mers, "between the two seas".

The right bank, cooler in winter and warmer in summer, dominated by the Merlot and Cabernet Franc, is a land of small estates, farmhouses and rolling hills. By complete contrast, the left bank is largely Cabernet Sauvignon country. This is flat, open land with large estates and huge areas of vineyard. Even here, however, the Cabernet Sauvignon never rules alone: it is always blended with the region's other red grape varieties; this is partly due to its history in the region – it was introduced later than the other grape varieties – and partly because here, by itself, it makes wines which are too tannic, too astringent.

The appellation system of Bordeaux has a number of levels which, as they refer to an increasingly small area, also refer to higher quality wines. At one end of the scale are the region-wide appellations of Bordeaux and, higher in alcohol (but not necessarily in quality), Bordeaux Supérieur. Great swathes of vineyard outside the more famous villages and districts are covered by these two appellations. They provide the basis for wines labelled (in Britain) as claret, or with the brand name of merchants or supermarkets. Many of the thousands of small wine estates – known in the wine trade as *petits châteaux* – in these peripheral vineyards can produce very acceptable, inexpensive reds or whites; the problem is how to sort the good from the bad. Buying from a good wine merchant or supermarket can relieve this problem – and when buying on the spot, advice from local shops can help.

Once inside the outer ring of basic Bordeaux, the roll call of famous district and village names begins. First, there are district appellations – on the left bank, the red wine vineyards of Médoc and Haut-Médoc, and the red and dry white wine land of Graves. Between the rivers, the district appellation of Entre-Deux-Mers produces dry white wines.

On the right bank, where divisions are smaller, there are no large districts – instead there are village appellations. Here Pomerol produces fat, juicy wines from the Merlot, while Saint-Emilion has more perfumed, supple wines made from the Cabernet Franc.

Rich, voluptuous wines – especially the Pomerol – require rich food, in contrast to the Cabernet Sauvignon wines from the Médoc, for which meat dishes in a simpler, "English" style are suitable.

Each of these two villages has its satellites, neighbouring hamlets which like to bask in the lustre of the big names by adding them to their own: the village appellations Saint-Georges-Saint-Emilion, Montagne-Saint-Emilion, Lalande-de-Pomerol –

cheaper wines, but also of less good quality.

Just to the west, the wines of Fronsac and Canon-Fronsac are firm, tannic when young, with a proportion of Malbec grapes in the blend which give colour and mouth-filling fruit. Until very recently, these wines represented good value – now fame has, regrettably, forced their price to catch up with their quality. But value is still to be found in the neighbouring vineyards of the Côtes de Bourg, where quantities of fruity, youthful, enjoyable wine are made; and, to a lesser extent, in Blayais, where the appellation Premières Côtes de Blaye produces some decent reds – youthful and supple wines which mature quickly.

On the road east of Saint-Emilion are other small appellations: Côtes de Castillon probably holds the red wine with the best future – quality is improving – although Côtes de Francs has some good estates.

On the left bank, the villages of the Médoc contain the greatest estates in Bordeaux, with wines of great complexity and longevity: Saint-Estèphe, Pauillac, Saint-Julien, Margaux, and the smaller villages of Moulis and Listrac. In the Graves there is one village appellation: Pessac-Léognan.

In these villages are the estates classified as First Growths – amongst them Margaux, Lafite-Rothschild, Latour and Mouton-Rothschild. This classification took place in 1855, when the great red wines of the Médoc were divided into five levels of quality, by estate – each one labelled from Premier to Cinquième Cru according to the price of its wines. The only other wine considered worthy of classification was that from Château Haut-Brion, a Graves estate, and these designations, almost without exception, remain intact today.

In the same year, the wine estates of Sauternes were classified into First and Second Growths (Premiers and Deuxièmes Crus), apart from one – Château d'Yquem – which was given the superior standard of Grand Premier Cru, and it is still true that those classified estates make the best wines.

But if these top wines are beyond the reach of most of us, the great strength of Bordeaux is that there are wines that can suit all pockets. For once, quality and, on the whole, reliability, go together.

▼ *The vineyards and* chai *(storehouse) of Château d'Yquem in Sauternes, producer of famous dessert wines.*

BORDEAUX AND THE SOUTHWEST

OTHER SPECIALITIES OF THE REGION AND WINES TO TRY WITH THEM

While the cuisine of the Bordelais proper is comparatively poor, the region is bordered by two of the richest culinary areas in France. To the south is Gascony, home of Armagnac brandy, of rich *confits* and *foie gras*, of Madiran and Pacherenc du Vic Bilh wines: impressively deep-coloured reds, often tannic and long-lived, and rich, honeyed whites. To the east lies Périgord, with the ancient vineyards of Cahors and the densely black truffle.

▲ Lamproie à la bordelaise *and its essential ingredient and accompaniment.*

As has happened in other regions in France, a method of cooking developed locally has broadened in influence and is now copied the world over. Dishes **à la bordelaise** are cooked or served with a wine sauce containing shallots, garlic and parsley (bone marrow and mushrooms may also be included). Either red or white wine can be used in the sauce, which may accompany either fish or meat. Perhaps the most truly regional of these dishes is **lamproie à la bordelaise**, made with lampreys, but beef is frequently used. For **entrecôte à la bordelaise**, the steak is traditionally grilled over the embers of vine cuttings before the sauce is added.

To drink: *a red with some tannin, perhaps from the Médoc or Graves.*

A hearty meal at harvest time is a feature of every wine region. The Bordeaux grape pickers fill up with **soupe des vendangeurs**. Quantities of meat (pork and ham) and root vegetables (carrots, onions and leeks) in a meaty stock, soaked up with liberal amounts of bread, and with plenty of quaffing red wine, go far in helping the next round of back-breaking work in the vineyard.

To drink: *an appellation Bordeaux, or any inexpensive red Bordeaux.*

Chabrot is a tradition which goes hand in hand with soup-making in the southwest. Just before a plate of soup is finished, a little red wine is poured into it, and the dish is then drained.

At one time, a cast iron cooking pot known as a *tourtière* would have been found on every hearth throughout the region. Few remain today, but the name survives for pies and pastries which would once have been cooked in it, such as **tourtière de poulet aux salsifis** (chicken and salsify pie). The chicken is marinated with herbs and white wine, then cooked with baby onions and salsify in puff pastry.

To drink: *a wine with some tannin as well as fruit – a red such as a Médoc or perhaps a Cahors.*

The cooking of both Périgord and Gascony are greatly indebted to the goose and the duck, and not just for *foie gras*. **Alicot** is a rural dish from Béarn, in the far southwest: a ragout made with the giblets and wings of geese, ducks or turkeys, casseroled with haricot beans, garlic, mushrooms and red wine. The name for this dish is taken from the words *ailles cuites*, literally "cooked wings".

And there is **cou d'oie farci** (goose neck stuffed with *foie gras*), or

▲ *Hams from the Landes are almost as famous as those of Bayonne.*

the versatile **confit de canard** and **confit d'oie**, which employ an ancient method of keeping meat: the salted duck or goose flesh is cooked slowly and then preserved in its own fat in sealed tins or stoneware jars. The meat has lost none of its flavour when it is removed from the jar – and can be eaten either hot or cold.

To drink: *the choice lies between a sweet white wine, such as a young Sauternes or a Monbazillac, or a mature red, perhaps a Saint-Emillion, a Fronsac or a Côtes de Castillon.*

Ttoro, a fish stew from the Pays Basque, resembles the Provençal *bouillabaisse*. As with other staple rural dishes, this one was invented to be practical as well as delicious, helping to make bony or less pleasantly textured fish more appetizing to eat. Today *ttoro* contains a variety of fish: conger eel, gunard, monkfish and hake, often garnished with mussels or langoustines. Chunks of the fish are cooked gently in oil and then added to a concentrated, highly-flavoured fish stock, or *fumet*, containing tomatoes, red peppers, chilli, garlic and lashings of white wine.

To drink: *the Bordelaise might drink a dry white Jurançon, a spicy and slightly tart wine.*

Jambon de Bayonne, Bayonne's salt-cured ham, has been a prized delicacy for over 500 years. Often eaten raw in thin slices, it also appears in vegetable and meat dishes, and in thick meaty soups.

To drink: *a red from Madiran, a white from Pacherenc du Vic Bilh, or a white Jurançon; the style should be full and not too acid for the whites, tough and fairly tannic for the reds.*

A classic dish from the southwest which includes Bayonne ham is the creamy and light **pipérade** – "*piper*" being the Béarnais name for sweet pepper. Lightly beaten egg is added to a stew of tomatoes, peppers and onions, and then scrambled as it is stirred into the vegetables. Diced ham can be added at the same time, or the finished dish can be topped with a slice of ham, fried or warmed.

To drink: *a light, fruity rosé from Béarn or Irouléguy.*

Truffles are the luxury dish of Périgord. The black truffle, today increasingly difficult to find and therefore more and more expensive, can only be bought fresh between November and March. If you are lucky enough to have the opportunity, the classic – and simplest – way of eating one is to wrap the truffle in bacon and cook it in the cinders of the fire. Today, truffles are much more often seen as the supreme ingredient of a stuffing or sauce.

To drink: *the delicate perfume of a truffle should never be overwhelmed; I believe the best partner is a lighter red, such as a mature Graves, although some people prefer the smoother, more opulent style of a Pomerol or Fronsac. A less expensive wine, such as a Côtes du Marmandais or Buzet, would be a good alternative.*

Despite the richness of the savoury dishes, there always seems to be room for one of the pastries and sweet dishes that are a speciality of the southwest. Périgord is famous for its marzipan and from Bayonne, via Spain, comes **touron**: a chequered almond paste square. Fruit tarts (apple and prune is a particular favourite in Gascony) are commonly found, and Gascony makes a speciality of crystallized fruits – the most famous are made with the **pruneaux** (prunes) from the town of Agen.

To drink: *with the French liking for dry sparkling wines with sweets, it's not uncommon to find champagne at this point in a meal in Gascony and Bordeaux. But, to be truly local, a sparkling Gaillac could be chosen.*

▼ *Fruit tarts and Barsac – a favourite combination in Bordeaux.*

BURGUNDY

It's a crisp spring evening. Outside, a full moon shines from a cloudless sky. In the huge banqueting hall of the Château de Gilly, a log fire burns at one end, thick tapestries hang from the pale yellow stone walls. Rows of tables gleam with cutlery, plates, bottles of wine and glasses. Along one side, an immense table is covered with rich fare for a cold night: quiches, hams from the hills of the Morvan – some baked in pastry, some as *jambon persillé* – rabbit *confit*, *pâté*, *saucisson, foie gras*. Large loaves and pale gold pats of butter stand ready to assist in the consumption of this impressive feast. More bottles of wine stand by for an even greater enchantment of the senses.

To a Rip van Winkle waking from a sleep that started in the Middle Ages, it would be a familiar scene. This is how it must have been in the days when the Duchy of Burgundy was poised to take over the Kingdom of France, when Dijon was the capital of a dominion that stretched from the Netherlands down to the south of France. And, although Burgundy is now a loyal region of the French republic, there's still a certain swagger to a Burgundian feast, a sense of profusion that reflects the rich larder of Burgundy's countryside – from the verdant pastures of the Saône Valley floor to the hillside vineyards of the Côte d'Or – and recalls the region's glorious past.

That it is, in fact, a dinner to add the finishing touch to a sumptuous tasting of wines from the neighbouring vineyard of Clos de Vougeot shows how firmly food and wine are linked in the Burgundian heart and mind. Food is used to celebrate wine – wine is seen as a natural extension of food.

Feasts themselves – the word seems more apt than mere "banquet" or "dinner" – are an inescapable part of Burgundy's wine culture. Many wine-lovers will have seen pictures of the elaborate rituals that accompany the great tastings at the château of the Clos de Vougeot: the impressive processions of robed initiates, the trumpet fanfares, then the singing of songs in praise of wine, large quantities of which are simultaneously being consumed. To a Burgundian, the enjoyment of feasting is a very serious matter.

The region's prime location, stretching north–south through the centre of France, made it an early cultural leader in the culinary arts; and the powerful political role it once had is still reflected in a confident and robust cuisine with strong flavours, vigorous sauces and lashings of wine and cream and garlic. The Burgundian vineyard forms a

▼ *The restaurant of the Château de Gilly, a worthy setting for medieval feasting.*

◄ *An ancient winepress at the Clos de Vougeot – a reminder that Burgundy favours traditional winemaking*

long, thin archipelago of four individual areas. The Clos de Vougeot is on the Côte de Nuits, the northern half of the Côte d'Or – so named because in autumn the vineleaves make the slopes glow with a blaze of colour. The southern half, or Côte de Beaune, gives way to the second area, the Côte Chalonnaise and this, in turn, leads down to the Mâconnais. Stranded on its own to the north is the island of Chablis.

The Domaine Rossignol-Trapet lies in some of

▲ *The courtyard of the Hôtel-Dieu in Beaune is a flamboyant statement of Burgundy's self-confidence.*

the very best wine country, in Gevrey-Chambertin on the Côte de Nuits. Sunday lunch with the family has much the same feel of royal – even biblical – enjoyment encountered at the Château de Gilly; it is a feast in a different guise.

The comfortable house nestles between its vineyard and its cellars – from where I had just returned from tasting some of the domain's recent vintages: village wines from Morey-Saint-Denis and Gevrey-Chambertin, a Premier Cru Gevrey-Chambertin and a Grand Cru, Chambertin; wines of great quality, depth and intensity. All the wines are the product of the domain's own vineyards, and typically for Burgundy these are tiny parcels of immeasurably valuable land – a few rows here, a few rows there. Now, over lunch, it is time to see how some older wines stand up to the abundance of classic Burgundian fare that Mme Rossignol-Trapet produces from her minute kitchen.

To start, a huge tranche of *foie de canard* (duck liver *pâté*) with truffles and a glass of Latricières-Chambertin 1980, a Grand Cru. Contrary to the popular belief that wine producers drink their best wines all the time, this is obviously a great treat for the family as well, and we discuss how the still youthful red has enough tannin and acidity to contrast with the dense, rich *pâté*, and how an older wine would not be structured enough.

A second Latricières-Chambertin is poured – this time from the great 1978 vintage, one of those magnificent years in which the wines could easily outlive the producers. This is still hugely full of fruitiness, deep in colour, and obviously marching gloriously on into the next century.

▼ *The new cellars of Domaine Rossignol-Trapet house wines from tiny parcels of immeasurably valuable land.*

The big wine copes well with the *tour-de-force* then set before us: *épaule de porc à la lie* – shoulder of pork cooked in a sauce of wine lees – Chambertin in this case, but Mme Rossignol-Trapet assures me that most richly-perfumed red wines would be suitable. The dish is a labour of love: the meat has been marinated for three days in the wine with locally grown thyme, onions and garlic, and then cooked slowly for four hours that morning. At the end, the juices of the meat and the marinade have been reduced to a creamy but not too thick sauce, which is served separately to be poured over the meat.

The cliché about food melting in the mouth has never been more appropriate, but does the richness of this dish, I wonder, allow the wine to speak, or simply overwhelm its character. The problem of imbalance between the region's food and its wine recurs again and again in Burgundy, and is articulated by Jean-Pierre de Smet, owner of Domaine de l'Arlot in Prémeaux near Nuits-Saint-Georges. He's a southerner, from Provence, and working hard to build up the reputation of his newly-acquired domain. Not being Burgundian, he can look at this sensitive issue dispassionately.

"It's all to do with the change in style that Burgundy wines have gone through in the last two decades. Recently, there's been more emphasis on fruit and perfume, less on tannin and power. The Pinot Noir" – M de Smet is in red wine territory on the Côte de Nuits – "ought to make a delicate wine, and the character of the cuisine should

▼ *A simple vigneron's lunch in Burgundy: bread, cheese and ham. Perhaps the wines are in a different class.*

reflect this. The older style of cooking was designed for hefty wines, fewer and fewer of which exist. In fact, the change has already been made, and cooking has now adapted to the lighter wines, with sauces that are less heavy and concentrated."

And yet, while that may be true of restaurants, in traditional households Burgundian cooking remains resolutely designed for the bitterly cold winters rather than the short, intensely hot summers. It also remains one of the most staunchly self-sufficient of the great French regional cuisines.

From the rivers and pastures of the wide Saône and Doubs valleys come freshwater fish and wildfowl, prime cattle and cereal crops, fruits – apples, pears, cherries from Saint-Bris in the Yonne – and vegetables – asparagus from Auxerre, leeks, pumpkins and haricot beans. Game and goats' milk cheese are brought down from the Morvan hills, to the west of the Côte d'Or, wild mushrooms populate the forests – in all, a wealth of ingredients that

◄ *Ancient, crumbling farm buildings show clearly how harsh and toilsome life can be for the French farmer.*

has formed the basis of local cuisine for centuries.

Of course this self-sufficiency was not only a virtue but a necessity. The region lies away from the great trading routes of the Rhine and the Rhône, and far from the ocean or sea. Transport, until the arrival of canals, and later the railway, was dependent upon unreliable, unsafe roads. Burgundians had to be resourceful and make do with the raw materials they had to hand.

To many outside France, some of these native

◄ *Some still prefer to lead an isolated existence in the remote, wooded countryside of the Morvan hills, west of the Côte d'Or.*

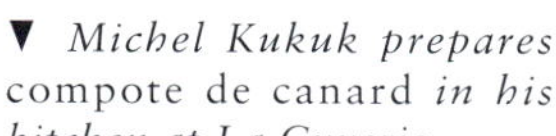

▼ *Michel Kukuk prepares* compote de canard *in his kitchen at La Cuverie.*

Compote de Canard

COMPOTE OF DUCK

A recipe from Michel Kukuk, chef-proprietor of La Cuverie restaurant in Savigny-lès-Beaune. He specializes in traditional Burgundian dishes – this one dates from the Middle Ages, when it was cooked on local farms. As with so much Burgundian fare, the recipe demands a bottle of expensive wine, but a cheaper Mâcon Rouge or Mercurey would be ideal as an ingredient and as an accompaniment. Whatever wine is chosen, it should be soft and rich, not too tannic.

Serves: 6 people

Preparation time: 30 minutes

Cooking time: 2¾ hours

1 duck, dressed and ready to cook, cut into 12 pieces

plain flour

duck fat

1 bottle good red burgundy

thyme

1 tbsp tomato purée (available in shops)

500g (1lb 2oz) new carrots, sliced

1 tsp granulated sugar

65g (2½oz) butter

salt, pepper

For the sauce

2 rashers bacon, diced into small cubes

16 small white onions, peeled

45g (1½oz) small, firm mushrooms

Preheat the oven to 180°C (350°F, gas mark 4). Coat the pieces of duck in flour. Heat a little duck fat in a frying pan and, on a high heat, seal the pieces all over.

Put the meat in a casserole dish and pour over the wine. Season with salt, pepper and thyme, and stir in the tomato purée. Place the dish in the oven and cook for 1½ hours.

Ten minutes before the end, heat the bacon in a frying pan. Add the onions, whole, and the mushrooms, halved or quartered.

Cook gently until the mushrooms and onions are soft, then add them to the casserole dish and cook for a further hour, by which time the sauce will have thickened. Stir occasionally to prevent burning.

Meanwhile, make a carrot purée by boiling the carrots in water with the sugar and 15g/½oz of butter until soft. Force through a sieve or mix in a blender. Heat the purée in a pan, adding some of the water the carrots were cooked in if it is too thick. Stir in the rest of the butter.

Place the pieces of duck on the carrot purée and pour the sauce over the top, serving any remaining sauce separately. Traditionally the dish would have been eaten with small boiled potatoes, but M Kukuk prefers boiled rice and chicory, cooked simply in boiling water.

◄ *Garlic hangs out to dry, ready for use in almost any Burgundian recipe.*

ingredients are the stuff of music hall jokes. Take snails. *Escargots* are a major delicacy in Burgundy, either in their shells or out – when they look like dark lumps of mushroom – and they always come smothered with pungent garlic sauce. In fact, snail by itself has a delicate taste of rather rubbery chicken and the reason you are eating it is because it gives you the chance to indulge in the God-given right every Burgundian claims: to eat considerable quantities of garlic.

Snails have been a staple of the Burgundian diet since man first arrived in the region. Deep in the southern Mâconnais the huge Rock of Solutré towers above the vineyards of Pouilly and Fuissé. Prehistoric man used to drive animals over this rock to their deaths and then climb down to the feast. Huge quantities of bones found at the foot of the Rock testify to this and, intermingled with these, were thousands of snail shells. Whether man enjoyed the snails as much as the venison is questionable – it may have been that when the pursuit was unsuccessful he was forced to eat these more complaisant creatures. It is certain that a taste for snails with garlic and other herbs dates back to Roman times – as shown in the illustrations on a 3rd century plate discovered at Sens.

Wine with snails is also an age-old combination.

► *Snails and wine made a quick combination in earlier days, when snails were plucked straight from the vineyard.*

Traditionally, snails were plucked from the vineyard after a shower of rain and enjoyed with a glass of white wine. Modern vineyard pesticides, fungicides and fertilizers have caused this shy creature to disappear and most snails are now raised on special farms. But spring is still the season for fresh snails, and you can see them in the markets of Beaune or Chalon-sur-Saône in huge tubs, crawling in convoluted heaps – although French housewives often find it more convenient to buy them ready-prepared, in tins.

Another traditional Burgundian delicacy also now comes in prepared form. Gone are the days when a pig would be an essential member of every Burgundian household, every ounce of it put to good use. And yet, although charcuterie plays a more important role a little further south in Lyon, one item made from pork – the *andouille* – is seen

Escargots à la Bourguignonne

SNAILS A LA BOURGUIGNONNE

A classic dish, often served as an entrée. The snails should be eaten piping hot with slices of fresh bread. A mature red wine, or one with good body and tannin, is an ideal drink.

Serves: 4 people

Preparation time: 40 minutes (plus 2 hours soaking time)

Cooking time: 3 hours 10 minutes

4 dozen snails, live or tinned

salt

For the garnish

30cl (10fl oz) white wine (a Chablis or Mâcon Blanc would be ideal)

60cl (1pt) water

2 shallots, chopped

1 bouquet garni

1 garlic clove, chopped

5cl (2fl oz) *marc de Bourgogne*

salt, pepper

For the butter stuffing

2 garlic cloves, chopped

2 shallots, chopped

chopped parsley

350g (12oz) butter

salt, pepper

For live snails: wash the snails and leave covered in water with a good handful of salt for at least 2 hours. Rinse in fresh water and then cook in boiling water for 6 minutes. Remove the snails from their shells and rinse in fresh cold water. Snip the black part from the end of the tail and put the snails to one side. Dry the shells in a warm oven.

For tinned snails: rinse the snails in warm water, cook for 5 minutes in boiling water and then continue as above.

Prepare the garnish by putting the wine, water, shallots, bouquet garni and garlic in a pan, with a seasoning of salt and pepper. Pour over the *marc de Bourgogne* and leave to simmer on a very low heat for 3 hours until the mixture has a thick buttery consistency.

Preheat the oven to 200°C (400°F, gas mark 6). Prepare the butter stuffing by mixing together the garlic, shallots, parsley and butter. Season with salt and pepper. Stir the mixture into the garnish, leaving a little of the garnish on one side.

Brush the empty shells with the remaining garnish. Put a piece of the butter into each shell, place the snails back in the shells and seal each one with some more butter.

Place the shells on an ovenproof dish and heat in the oven for 2–3 minutes until the butter begins to bubble and and the garnish has given the snail shells a sheen.

Serve immediately.

▲ *Produce from smallholdings in the Saône Valley is sold daily outside the Hôtel-Dieu in Beaune.*

as a great delicacy in Burgundy. This sausage is made from the pig's stomach, cut into strips, salted, enclosed in a skin and preserved in brine. It is sold uncooked, but charcutiers in Beaune dry it, giving it the appearance of an old, shrivelled club or stick. Forget the looks is the general advice; think about the taste, which, once it has been soaked in water for a couple of days, cooked slowly and served with white haricot beans, elevates it beyond its origins in peasant fare.

Andouille bourguignonne appears on the menu of many of Burgundy's Michelin-starred restaurants. Opinion divides over the best wine to accompany it: red or white, Côte de Nuits or Côte de Beaune. I find that the slightly salty character of the dish, and the richness of the beans suggests a good strong, not too aristocratic white wine, perhaps from further south on the Côte Chalonnaise or in the Mâconnais.

The partnering of Burgundian food with the region's wine was the topic under discussion with Mme Potel, of Domaine de la Pousse d'Or in

Volnay. I arrived late and Gérard, her husband, was rushing to take his turn in supervising the village polling station for the local elections. So we dashed through a tasting of wines in the domain's medieval cellars – Pommards, Santenays and Volnays, the soft velvety Volnays contrasting with the perfumed, earthy Santenays and the firmer Pommards.

Then it was over to the house and into a room which must have the best view in Burgundy – across a sweep of some of the most expensive

◄ *Every shop offers the visitor an* embarras de richesse *in Burgundy, there is so much good food to choose from.*

vineyards – from Pommard to Meursault, and, right in front, the walled vineyard of Bousse d'Or. The fact that it was raining meant that the panorama – "on a really clear day you can see the Alps" – was not forthcoming, but it did mean that logs were burning in the large stone fireplace and a warming glass of *marc de Bourgogne*, the local grape spirit, could be offered.

Mme Potel, elegant and relaxed even after cooking Sunday lunch for the family, made an immediate distinction between wines from "big" years and those from "light" years. For her, wines from the greater vintages, with the classic Pinot Noir tendency towards sweetness, coupled with tannins – and, with maturity, ripe gamey flavours – are more suited to chicken or game dishes, ones in which the sauce or meat is sweet. They suit the very rich meat dishes, marinated meats, or wild boar. By contrast, wines from lighter years taste better with pork and veal, because the greater acidity of the wine counterpoints the delicate taste of the meat.

As with Domaine Rossignol-Trapet, this is a red wine-only household (even with desserts), and so we searched for a suitable wine to partner Burgundy's freshwater fish – the carp, salmon, pike, trout and eel – netted from the Saône and its tributaries, and from the mountain streams of the Morvan, which feed into the Loire. "Santenay, from the Côte de Beaune", said Mme Potel, firmly. "Its earthy taste and fruit would go very well." The red wines of Mercurey on the Côte Chalonnaise would be another choice. The secret of their success is

▼ *The pedestrianized centre of Beaune offers plenty of opportunities to eat and drink the local produce.*

► *A selection of* fromages de chèvre *– goats' milk cheese – either mild and fresh or mature, with a strong, rustic flavour.*

▼ *Unpasteurized cheeses reign supreme in this Beaune* fromagerie. *Some of those which are* à point *(ready to eat) are runny enough to need support from plastic containers.*

the comparative lack of tannin, the softness of these wines. With the bigger, bolder wines of the Côte d'Or, the tannins would be exaggerated by the taste of the fish.

Although Burgundy is far inland, fish plays a surprisingly important part in the diet. River fish were plentiful at one time, but today they may be imported or even farmed, especially trout. Yet ancient recipes are still handed down – Mme Rossignol-Trapet cooks *pochouse* from a recipe first recorded in 1598 in Chalon-sur-Saône. This substantial stew is bursting with every imaginable river fish; these are doused with white wine and plenty of garlic, and crisp garlic bread croûtons are added at the last minute to soak up some of the juices. A local variation, for added punch, includes a glass of *marc de Bourgogne*, the region's brandy.

The Burgundian cheeseboard is always, even in private houses, the centrepiece of a meal, but the successful combination of Burgundy's cuisine with its red wines becomes more problematic here. Mature red wines suffer against any type of cheese, which is a pity because it is generally at this point in a meal that older vintages are opened.

Cheese production is a serious business in Burgundy and a stroll around the pedestrianized centre of medieval Beaune reveals that the local demand has, happily, ignored any advice to cut down on cholesterol.

My first experience with the Burgundian cheeseboard, many years ago, was, quite literally, explosive. There were, of course, several cheeses in front of me that are found in every region of France, and in every country of the world, such as Camembert, Brie and Roquefort.

But on pointing at strange shapes – evil-looking red-coloured lumps, and black-coated pyramids – I discovered that there are cheeses of every sort native to Burgundy. There is the creamy, gently spicy, blue-veined Bleu de Bresse, ash-covered Chaource (also produced in Champagne), and Epoisses, a cheese cured either in red wine or in Chablis and strong enough when first tasted to make me reach for a healing glass of water and pause for consideration.

Such assertive cheeses are not happy partners for the smooth wines of Burgundy, but the very much more local cheeses, made from cows' milk: the Amour de Nuits, from Nuits-Saint-Georges, or its counterpart from Gevrey-Chambertin, the savoury L'Ami du Chambertin do marry well. Even better – and probably the best match with red burgundy – is the soft and deliciously creamy Cîteaux.

It comes as something of a surprise to learn that the mother monastery of the Cistercian order is alive and going strong about four miles from Nuits-Saint-Georges. Lying in the middle of rich farming country near the River Doubs, a series of large barrack-like buildings stands behind pairs of firmly closed gates. Today the monks still draw on their land of milk (they probably make honey as well!) to produce Cîteaux cheese. Looking at the countryside, it is perfectly possible to understand how the easy life at one time overtook the monks: the fat of the land is all around, while not so far

Gougères

Light and delicate, these cheese choux pastry puffs go well with an apéritif such as a crisp Chablis or a red from the Côte Chalonnaise.

Serves: 4 people

Preparation time: 10 minutes

Cooking time: 50–55 minutes

25cl (8fl oz) water

100g (4oz) butter

150g (5oz) self-raising flour, sifted

4 eggs (size 2)

60g (2oz) Gruyère cheese, grated

45g (1½oz) Gruyère cheese, cut into small cubes

grated nutmeg

salt, pepper

Preheat the oven to 220°C (425°F, gas mark 7). Place the water, butter and a pinch of salt in a pan. Bring to the boil, draw off the heat and add the flour quickly, stirring rapidly until the mixture leaves the side of the pan.

Stir for about half a minute over the heat, then draw off the heat and add the eggs one by one, ensuring that the dough does not become too liquid, but has a soft consistency. Add the grated cheese, then the cubes of gruyère. Season with pepper and nutmeg.

Put dessertspoonfuls of the dough, well spaced out, on a non-stick baking tray in little balls or, using a piping bag, in the shape of crowns, to make about 25.

Place the tray in the oven and cook for 45 minutes, or until the *gougères* are brown and have risen. The cubes of Gruyère will have softened, leaving pockets of melted cheese inside the dough.

Serve immediately.

▲ Gougères, *featherweight pastries, are traditionally filled with Gruyère and served hot from the oven as appetizers.*

away are the finest vineyards of Burgundy.

For the region's stronger cheeses, even blue cheese – a white burgundy is best, especially one with some oak flavour (derived from the cask it matured in).

White wine appears less frequently in Burgundian cooking than red simply because, in much of the region, more red than white is produced; but go to Chablis or the Mâconnais and the balance is redressed. From the Mâconnais comes Fromage Fort – a powerful concoction of Fromage Frais laced with white wine and *marc de Bourgogne*, allowed to ferment for several days before being spread on small toasts. It is invariably eaten with a glass of the local white wine, preferably a fuller-flavoured Pouilly-Fuissé or a Saint-Véran.

Mme Potel believes that white wine is often better than red as a marinade for meats: it tenderizes the flesh, but leaves the flavours more prominent than a red wine. For many sauces, too, white wine is better than red, because of the softer, acids and lack of tannin in the whites – but the two dishes which many regard as Burgundy's greatest are both based on copious quantities of red wine.

Coq au vin and *boeuf bourguignon* bring together the rich produce of the plains and the fruit of the hills in perfect harmony. Poulets de Bresse, the chickens from the town of Bourg-en-Bresse, east of Mâcon, are reputedly the finest in France. So seriously is their quality taken, that they have their own appellation contrôlée and production is strictly controlled. There's no overcrowding here, with each chicken guaranteed a certain amount of land.

However, the recipe for *coq au vin* was originally devised to make old and stringy birds more palatable. Long, slow cooking of a bird that might have been running around the farmyard for a year or more – you still see plenty of them in rural Burgundy – ensured that the taste was preserved while the texture was softened. The sauce for *coq au vin* is itself cooked slowly, reduced for at least an hour, to give a full and concentrated flavour.

This method of preparation – the red wine sauce and garnish of mushrooms, tiny onions and diced bacon (*lardons*) – is so characteristic of Burgundian cuisine that it has become a culinary term: *à la bourguignonne*. It is used both for *coq au vin* and for *boeuf bourguignon*, but, historically, the latter dish has held quite a different status in the region's cuisine.

While chickens were fairly common on any farm, Charolais beef cattle were precious items, not to be sacrificed lightly. Indeed, the Charolais cattle are still considered one of the best breeds in France. Even today, in parts of Burgundy like the rugged *massif* of the Morvan, where peasants are still poor, it is not unusual to see a farmer leading the farm's single cow.

So *boeuf bourguignon* was reserved for the annual saint's day or given, in the form of a thick soup,

▼ *Charolais cattle in the Saône Valley, living off the fat of some of the richest land in France.*

▲ *Rabbit with mustard and* crème fraîche *sauce, cooked by Mme Potel at Domaine de la Pousse d'Or.*

rather than a stew, to the ill and infirm as a sure and certain cure. But wine was always an essential ingredient – and it is quite likely that "*bourguignon*" refers to the wine used in the sauce, rather than to the region itself.

Good red burgundy is still the best accompaniment for this substantial dish. Certainly on a chilly spring night in Beaune, a plate of *boeuf bourguignon* served, unusually, with pasta (normally it would be simply served with boiled potatoes) and accompanied both with lashings of Dijon mustard and with several glasses of a rich, soft, mature Savigny-lès-Beaune, seems to yield up the essence of Burgundian cooking.

This is not the elaborate food of great palaces, the elegant cuisine that can be consumed by people with fastidious appetites, or those who are not really hungry. This is food that can satisfy a farmer or vigneron after a hard day's work, with copious helpings for healthy appetites, just as, in its time, it satisfied the knight back home from a day's robbing, pillaging or mere friendly jousting.

Lapin au Sauce Moutarde à la Crème Fraîche

RABBIT WITH MUSTARD AND CREME FRAICHE SAUCE

This recipe, from Mme Gérard Potel, brings in two of Burgundy's most famous ingredients: Dijon mustard and crème fraîche *– pasteurized cream which has had the fermenting agents returned to it, giving it a slightly cheesy or tart flavour.*

Dijon mustard has a long and impressive history. The word moutarde *was used as a pun in a motto of the Dukes of Burgundy. "Moult tarde" they used to cry: "the last to be made". Historians have long debated which came first, the name or the cry.*

Mustard was originally made either by using grape must (unfermented grape juice) or vinegar; but Dijon mustard is different and, Burgundians would claim, superior, because it uses verjus, *the juice extracted from under-ripe grapes.*

The dish gives the vigneron the satisfaction of eating one of the vineyard's major pests – rabbit – but most of us, of course, will buy rabbit ready-prepared. The dish goes well with a smooth red wine, a Côte de Beaune or Mercurey, or with a full-bodied oak-matured white.

Serves: 4 people

Preparation time: 10 minutes

Cooking time: 1 hour

2 whole rabbits, ready to cook

50g (2oz) butter

3 tbsp *crème fraîche*

2½ tbsp Dijon mustard

olive oil

salt, pepper

Preheat the oven to 200°C (400°F, gas mark 6). Baste the rabbits with olive oil, salt and pepper. Place them in a roasting dish with a little water to absorb the juices and roast in the oven for 1 hour, or until the skin is golden.

In the last quarter of an hour of cooking prepare the sauce. Melt the butter over a low heat, add the *crème fraîche* and stir in the mustard. Pour in enough of the juices from the roasting dish to make a medium-thick gravy and simmer gently until it has been reduced by half and has a smooth, thick consistency.

Cut up the rabbit with kitchen shears or carve into slices. Pour the sauce over the meat, or serve separately.

Mme Potel likes a simple accompaniment of boiled cabbage and potatoes for this dish.

WINES OF BURGUNDY

The wines of Burgundy are a true reflection of their region – open, welcoming, expansive, hedonistic, demanding enjoyment. They speak to the heart rather than the head. The experience of drinking fine burgundy is above all pleasurable: the wine sings in the glass, offering fellowship rather than elegance, a big hug rather than a limp handshake.

The taste of the reds, when young, can have intensely vibrant fruit flavours – raspberry and cherry – and, when mature, can yield the smoke of wood fires, the savour of game and even suggest rotting vegetables and manure. The whites, often opulent, show peaches, apricots, bananas even, mingling with oak, mellowing into liquid gold, luscious and rich.

That is the joy of burgundy. The problem is that searching for that joy, reaching to the heart of fine burgundy, can give rise to so many disappointments on the way, and can, in the end, cost so much, that some wine drinkers are driven away, feeling that burgundy is not for them, that they are not in the right league, that burgundy is a mystery.

The trouble lies with the way Burgundy is organized. It has the most complex system of appellations in France – the product of centuries of subdivision (in Burgundy all children inherit an equal share of the family property), and the result of land divided into minute parcels, and of villages jealously protecting their own reputation. The fact that, at the end of the day, Burgundy essentially produces only two wine styles – red from the Pinot Noir, white from the Chardonnay – albeit with infinite, subtle variations on these two themes – is

easily obscured and forgotten by foreign explorers.

The best advice for anyone wishing to sample Burgundy's wines is to buy from a good producer, regardless of the appellation – a sound suggestion in a region where most appellations are tiny, and the majority are divided between numerous producers, whose quality of wine can vary from the mediocre to the very good indeed.

Burgundy is a land of smallholdings. A producer may own just a couple of hectares of vines scattered in small plots between a number of different appellations, ranging perhaps from the most basic to a top Grand Cru. In this fragmented landscape, it becomes vital to consider the reputation and winemaking skills of an individual producer.

Take perhaps the most famous vineyard in Burgundy as an example. The Clos de Vougeot is a Grand Cru vineyard in the village of Vougeot on

◄ *Vineyard smallholdings may be centuries old. The invitation here to come and taste is implicit in the word "ici".*

◀ *Chambolle-Musigny in the heart of the Côte d'Or: a slender strip of vineyards runs between valley floor and hilltop.*

▼ *The vineyards of Ladoix-Serrigny. Every change in the direction of the rows indicates a change of owner.*

the Côte de Nuits – a single vineyard appellation in its own right. If this were Bordeaux, the Clos would have one owner, making one wine. Because this is Burgundy there are, at the latest count, 77 different producers all making wine called Clos de Vougeot. Great Clos de Vougeot should be a weighty wine, full of tobacco and plummy fruit, with a touch of new wood and tannin: a wine that can age and enrich itself over many years. And yet, a tasting of 22 of these wines at the 1992 spring festival, the Grands Jours de Bourgogne, suggested that about 10 per cent are worthy of the appellation and the price, leaving a great many wines, and producers, trading on a great name and debasing it.

So, buying Burgundy can seem as hazardous as stepping through a minefield. But, with a little work – not hard work – it is possible to approach the wines with confidence and be well rewarded.

Although the variety of different appellations can be confusing, the very basic division of Burgundy into four distinct regions is much easier to cope with. The long, thin vineyard of Burgundy starts in the north with the small white wine area of Chablis – a land of fish dishes and classic sauces – followed, after a large gap, by the narrow strip of vineyards which forms the Côte d'Or, itself divided between the Côte de Nuits and the Côte de Beaune, and the source of Burgundy's greatest wines. Here we find some of the most sumptuous and full-flavoured cooking in France to partner these rich wines – and indeed to employ them in sauces and marinades – the great beef casseroles, the fish stews, the pungent garlic and creamy cheeses. To the south, there are the larger areas of the Côte Chalonnaise and the Mâconnais before Burgundy merges into the Beaujolais. The cooking becomes lighter here, in tune with the more delicate wines, luxurious heaviness giving way to a gentler southern touch, with greater use of oil and less of butter.

In the time it takes to travel from Chablis to the southern Mâconnais, you will have left the cool

◄ *Maurice Pouleau picks blackcurrants in his garden at Rochepot to go into the local liqueur, Cassis.*

north and taken your first few steps into the warm south, with its promise of shady olive groves and life lived out of doors – a distance of more than 200 kilometres.

Despite the huge longitudinal distance involved, the climate of Burgundy is surprisingly homogeneous. The whole region is comparatively far north – the main vineyards of the Côte d'Or are well north of Bordeaux. As in Alsace, the climate is continental – the sea can have no ameliorating effect here – with savagely cold winters and scorchingly hot summers. The vineyards are in the rain shadow of the Massif Central, on the south-east-facing slopes of tree-topped hills which face across the Saône Valley towards the Alps. But there is regular rainfall during the spring and late autumn, and always, during the vital period of ripening, the chance of devastating hail storms which can ruin a small area's entire crop.

The weather can vary greatly from one year to the next, from years in which there are perfect growing conditions – a dry July and August followed by a warm, golden September – to rain-sodden, cold summers and dank autumns. What is more, a great year for red wines is not necessarily the best for whites – and vice versa. So, just to add a little spice to the complexity of burgundy, the character of each vintage must be taken into account.

It is, however, possible to trace a progression in the standard of Burgundy's wines. From the great vineyards in the north of the region – the Grands and Premiers Crus of Chablis and the Côte d'Or – the quality diminishes gently on the Côte Chalonnaise until you reach the uncomplicated wines of the Mâconnais.

The appellation system – even if complex – is organized with impeccable French logic. It works on the premise that the smaller the appellation, the finer should be the wine – which is perfectly true, all other things (such as the quality of the producer) being equal.

So the basic regional appellations – Bourgogne Rouge and Bourgogne Blanc, made from Pinot Noir and Chardonnay – are general and apply to the whole of Burgundy. There are other, lesser regional appellations – Bourgogne Passe-Tout-Grains, made from Pinot Noir and Gamay, and Bourgogne Aligoté, a crisp, tart, refreshing white made from the Aligoté grape.

One rung up from these Burgundy-wide appellations are regional appellations which cover a series of villages – such as Côte de Nuits-Villages, Hautes Côtes de Nuits and Côte de Beaune-Villages. These wines are often very good value, with softer, lighter fruit which develops quickly.

Moving up again are the village appellations. Most of the best Burgundian wine communes are entitled to their own appellation, even if not all the vineyards in the commune should lay claim to it. Typical village appellations are Vosne-Romanée or Nuits-Saint-Georges on the Côte de Nuits, or Savigny-lès-Beaune or Meursault on the Côte de Beaune, Mercurey on the Côte Chalonnaise, or Pouilly-Fuissé in the Mâconnais. Good village wines should have some concentration, with the ability to age, the whites over a decade, and the reds over many decades.

Certain vineyards in each village are regarded as making better wine than others and these will either be designated Premier Cru, the next level of quality – the wine label will specify the village as well as the name of the vineyard – or they will be Grand Cru, which are believed to produce the finest wine of all. These latter vineyards have their own, individual appellation.

Good (and famous) examples are Le Montrachet, Chambertin and Romanée-Conti. What sets Grand Cru wines apart is a combination of the vineyard's level of exposure – a vital factor in Burgundy – its position on the slope (half to two-thirds of the way up is considered best), the nature of the soil (it should be light and well-drained) and the human element – much less easy to quantify. If all these factors come together in their ideal form, you have a Grand Cru wine.

This brings us back to the producer – who may simply produce wines from his own vineyards, or may additionally buy in grapes or wine from other grape growers. The former are known as domains, the latter as négociants (merchants). And while négociants can be relied upon to produce reasonable quality in the lesser appellations (because of their ability to buy grapes or wine from anywhere in Burgundy), it is generally true that the domains are the star producers when it comes to the finest burgundies of all, having refined their techniques over a great many years of good husbandry and meticulous care in the *élevage*, or "bringing up", of the wine.

The domains are the true inheritors of tradition in Burgundy. Despite stainless steel in the cellars, Burgundy is a region where ancient customs and methods are still honoured – where the problems of land inheritance may have ossified development, but where the skill of the producer can affect the quality of the wine more forcibly than in any other wine region of France. It is this tantalizing – and infuriating – human element which can lead to some of the worst winemaking, but whose genius can also forge the world's greatest.

▼ *Pinot Noir vines in Aloxe-Corton on the Côte d'Or – for many, these grapes produce the finest red wines in the world.*

BURGUNDY

OTHER SPECIALITIES OF THE REGION AND WINES TO TRY WITH THEM

Burgundy has a cuisine of great depth and breadth. Here, superlative wines are met by superlative food in a powerful yet refined form – sustaining a centuries-old reputation for producing the culinary best.

The classic method of preparation in Burgundy is to cook the main ingredient – whether it be meat, fish, poultry or egg – in a red wine sauce, with baby onions, mushrooms and *lardons* (strips or cubes of bacon): in other words, **à la bourguignonne**.

To drink: *locally, these dishes are accompanied with the wine used in the sauce but, if this is basic "plonk", try a rich style of Pinot Noir from the Côte Chalonnaise or Côte d'Or.*

Dishes described as **en meurette** are cooked in a similar fashion; eggs are poached gently in red wine sauce for **oeufs en meurette**, then garnished with crisply fried croûtons. **Meurette de poisson** is a form of *matelote* (fish stew) – fresh-water fish including pike, trout, carp, perch and eel are casseroled in red wine.

To drink: *again, accompany with the wine used in cooking, or with a smooth red, low in tannin – a Mâcon Rouge.*

Easter is the traditional time to serve **jambon persillé**, a ham galantine – perhaps made with the excellent ham from the Morvan. The meat is cooked gently in white wine with onions, shallots, garlic and cloves, and then left to set in the strained cooking liquid. Delicious with a dab of Dijon mustard and a few pickled gherkins.

To drink: jambon persillé *often appears as the first course, with white wine – a Mâcon Blanc or a Chablis – but a soft red would also be suitable.*

Saupiquet, dating back to the 16th century, is a speciality of the Morvan and once again makes use of its ham. Slices are fried and served with a cream sauce enlivened with vinegar, shallots, tarragon and juniper berries.

To drink: *a lightly acid, quite rustic red, perhaps a Hautes Côtes de Nuits or Hautes Côtes de Beaune.*

With the usual economy of the rural cook, nothing was wasted from the family pig, in earlier days. **Ferchuse** was created to make use of the offal; the pieces are browned before being cooked in local red wine with stock, garlic and shallots.

To drink: *either the wine used in cooking, or a full-bodied red such as a Santenay or Côte Chalonnaise.*

Dishes **à la dijonnaise** allow the specialities of that city to come to the fore. The term refers to both sweet and savoury recipes: the savoury including mustard, the sweet blackcurrants. For **poussin à la moutarde** (chicken with mustard) the bird is covered with mustard and baked in a gratin dish, *crème fraîche* is poured over and the meat cooked further and then served with a sauce of the juices mixed with butter.

To drink: *either a rich white such as*

▼ *Long, slow cooking tenderizes the flesh of robust farmyard hens.*

a Meursault, the more acid style of Aligoté de Bouzeron, or a tannic red wine from Saint-Aubin, Saint-Romain or the Hautes Côtes.

Vegetable cultivation centres around Dijon and near Auxonne, to the east of the city, and includes beans, leeks, onions, pumpkin and artichokes. **Flammiche aux poireaux**, a leek tart made in Burgundy and Picardy, is a double-crusted pie; the leeks are cooked in butter until very soft, then seasoned and bound with egg yolk.

To drink: *a good, smooth white wine, perhaps one from the Côte Chalonnaise, or the lighter style found in the Mâconnais, in Pouilly-Fuissé or Saint-Véran.*

Rigodon was traditionally made at the end of baking day, cooked slowly in the oven's remaining heat. The dish can be prepared with ham or bacon – when it looks like a cross between a flan and an omelette – and served as an entrée. For this, ham is diced and sautéed, a seasoned mixture of egg, flour and milk is poured on top and the whole then baked in the oven until the liquid has set. Alternatively, *rigodon* can be cooked as a dessert and served cold with poached or puréed seasonal fruit. Red fruits make an attractive contrast to this pale, creamy pudding, which is made with *brioche* crumbs soaked in milk flavoured with cinnamon and vanilla, mixed with locally-grown hazelnuts and walnuts, and then baked gently.

▼ *A favourite ingredient of pâtissiers, but also good in home-made* clafoutis.

▲ *Cheeses here come large or small – the smallest aptly named "trouser button".*

To drink: *if the dish is savoury, a red such as a Mâcon Rouge would be suitable because not too overwhelming for the simplicity of the dish. If the* rigodon *is served with fruit, a Burgundian would probably drink a Crémant de Bourgogne.*

Sweet dishes in Burgundy frequently make use of local fruits. For **flamusse aux pommes**, layers of apple are laid on the bottom of a dish and batter poured over the top; similar is the **clafoutis**, found throughout central France, and popular when cherries are in season – Saint-Bris cultivates a famously-good variety.

To drink: *there are no local dessert wines, but try a Crémant de Bourgogne, or pause and have a glass of* marc de Bourgogne, *the local brandy, with coffee.*

Burgundy's blackcurrant produce is considered among the best in the world – especially **crème de cassis** liqueur, which can add an extra dimension to poached fruit dishes and sorbets. When mated with Burgundy's Aligoté wine it becomes Kir.

Superb cheeses are to be found in Burgundy. Lesser known varieties include the **Bouton-de-Culotte**, a tiny, sharp-tasting goats' milk cheese – its name means "trouser button". **Bressan** (from Bresse) is equally small – a cone-shaped goats' cheese; while the cows' milk **Saint-Florentin** is tangy and extremely soft. **Boulette de la Pierre-qui-Vire**, as **Cîteaux**, is made by Benedictine monks; the curds are sometimes flavoured with herbs.

To drink: *locals would drink the red wine which accompanied the main meat course, but strong-tasting cheeses can be better with white wine. Leave the reds for softer, smoother cheeses.*

CHAMPAGNE

The Montagne de Reims is hardly a mountain, more a low ridge with vines on the slopes and forest on the summit. Strung out along the ridge, about halfway up, is a line of little villages: slate roofs clustered around a squat church with a stumpy spire. To anybody with more than a passing interest in champagne, their names are resonant: Verzenay, Verzy, Mailly, Chamery, Rilly. From these villages come the great Pinot Noir wines that are blended with Chardonnay and Pinot Meunier to make the world's greatest sparkling wine.

The windmill at Verzenay, high on the slope, offers the best view of this tranquil landscape – a broad sweep of vines runs to the northwest, while behind you it curves around the Montagne to the southeast. At the base of the slope, the vineyards stop abruptly, giving way to fields of grain. In the distance, on the plain to the north, stands the city of Rheims, still dominated by the bulk of its Gothic cathedral, which is one of the finest in France.

That sharp line where the vineyards end marks a significant boundary. Beyond, there are no more vines; these are the most northerly in France. Further on, the natural product is beer. It is as important a dividing line as the one in Provence where the olive tree signals the change to a Mediterranean climate and terrain. That France can accommodate both these boundaries is proof of the country's great size and also points to the enormous variety of produce that can be found within its frontiers.

This northerly boundary explains much about Champagne, both as a wine and as a region. The French, neatly distinguishing through gender, talk of La Champagne, La Région de Champagne, to differentiate it from *le champagne*, *le vin de champagne*.

La Champagne stretches from the forests of the Ardennes in the north, which straddle the Belgian border, to touch the tip of Burgundy in the south and the Ile de France in the west. *Le champagne* – the wine – is the product of a region with bitterly cold winters, and summers that can be as variable as Britain's. The wine, even in the warmest years, is light and high in acids. Much as I enjoy Coteaux Champenois, the region's still wine, there is no doubt that here is wine destined to have bubbles and to be called champagne.

It is a quirk of vinous history that champagne – as a sparkling wine – was developed at all. Until the 17th century the wine of Champagne was a still, light table wine with a tendency to *pétillance* when bottled. Although legends like to credit a monk, Dom Pierre Pérignon, with the single-handed creation of champagne, it is more likely that a series of developments had, by the early years of the 19th century, taken advantage of the local wine's natural character to make a sparkling wine – one whose influence and following was to leave its home region far behind.

So, because the region's principal wine is now champagne, rather than the original, still wine, the link between wine and authentic, regional cooking in Champagne is more tenuous than in other parts of France; their partnership is not a long-standing one. Champagne is a cosmopolitan wine, more suited to today's international, three-star cuisine than to the sort of home cooking that marries with the wines, say, of Burgundy or Provence.

But it would be wrong to dismiss local cuisine here as poor in resources, or limited in scope.

► *The valley of the Marne: Champagne can seem like a monocultural region, dominated by valuable vineyards.*

► *The stately house of Bollinger in Ay, typical of the solid prosperity of a region founded on long-term wealth.*

CHAMPAGNE BOLLINGER

Rather, the traditional cuisine has been outstripped in its pretensions by the local wine. It is quite possible to eat local dishes, drink local wine and find as happy a marriage between the two as in any other part of France. Not only are there plenty of local dishes whose flavours are enhanced by a glass of champagne – or, indeed, of Coteaux Champenois – but specialities have also been created to act as foils to champagne.

The pretty, vanilla-flavoured Biscuit Rose, made by Biscuit Fossier in Rheims, is just such a speciality. The original biscuit, created 200 years ago, was white and without the vanilla flavouring – a style still made today and called the Véritable Biscuit Fossier. When the vanilla-flavoured style was introduced in the early 19th century, a dash of pink colouring was added as a distinguishing mark.

To walk into the discreet premises of Biscuit Fossier on the Boulevard Jamin is to step back two centuries in time. In one corner, a large wood-burning oven is at work cooking the hand-made biscuits. Afterwards they will be dried out slowly in a space beneath the oven for three hours, to give a crisp, sweet biscuit tasting rather like the British sponge finger.

Considering it was created when champagne was a sweeter wine than it is now (the dry or *brut* style was not developed until the late 19th century) this light biscuit still goes surprisingly well with a glass mid-morning. Somehow the vanilla lessens the biscuit's sweetness and is enhanced by the champagne's dryness, especially, according to M Olivier, the manager, if the champagne is old and therefore less green. A *demi-sec* would have been chosen in the 18th and early 19th centuries and I would still recommend one today.

Although I doubt whether much has changed at Biscuit Fossier in over forty years, there is at least a gas-fired oven, through which other cakes and biscuits pass on a conveyor belt: the lovely spice and honey cakes called *pain d'épices*, and *croquignoles*, small, very light finger biscuits topped with a

dab of lurid icing. Macaroons called *marzepans* are piped onto trays before being cooked in a little hot-air oven.

The cold winters and austere climate probably account for the popularity of sweet foods in Champagne. A walk around Rheims or Epernay reveals numerous pâtisseries, doubling less as cafés than as coffee houses or *salons de thé*, bringing to mind the towns of central Europe. On a cold winter's day they are thronged with customers taking coffee and cakes in the morning, tea and cakes in the afternoon, filling the air with idle gossip and steaming up the windows.

I've found the finest *pain au chocolat* in France in Rheims' Place Drouet d'Erlon and, not far away in Rue Cérès, are the beautifully preserved 18th century premises of Chocolaterie Deleans. The shop's high-ceilinged, pale blue and white interior is designed to echo the Petit Trianon at Versailles, with gleaming mirrors, dainty shelves and counter display cases from which emanate the most

◄ *The Biscuit Rose (in the pink packets), partner for a morning glass of champagne, is part of a range which includes* pain d'épices *and* croquignoles.

Potée Champenoise

CHAMPENOIS STEW

Firmly part of Champagne's culinary heritage, potée champenoise *is a type of* pot-au-feu *or stew and is traditionally eaten by grape pickers at harvest time. This filling and substantial dish is just what is needed when work in the vineyard has started - often in cold, wet weather – at eight o'clock in the morning.*

Different meats are included, depending upon availability, although pork – the region's most important variety – is always an ingredient. All the meats in the recipe must be cooked in one piece, not sliced. The local practice is to serve the stock formed during cooking separately, as a first course like a soup and to serve the meat and vegetables afterwards. I would drink a soft, fruity, red Coteaux Champenois, or a full, rich, rosé champagne with this.

Serves: 8 people
Preparation time: 30 minutes (plus 12 hours soaking time)
Cooking time: 3 hours 20 minutes
450g (1lb) salted breast of pork
675g (1½lb) salted shoulder of pork
125g (4½oz) dried haricot beans
450g (1lb) shin of beef
450g (1lb) silverside of beef
half a chicken, jointed
450g (1lb) carrots, cut in half lengthways
1kg (2lb 4oz) savoy cabbage, chopped roughly
450g (1lb) turnips or parsnips (not both), cut in thick slices
1kg (2lb 4oz) leeks, cut in large chunks
450g (1lb) spicy sausage
450g (1lb) boiling potatoes, halved or quartered
salt, pepper

Soak the pork and haricot beans separately in water overnight. The following day, drain the pork and beans. Put all the meat, except the chicken and sausage, in a large saucepan. Cover with water and bring to the boil over a moderate heat. Skim the fat which rises to the top while simmering (this takes 15–20 minutes, but must be done thoroughly to prevent the dish from tasting too fatty). Cover and simmer for 1 hour.

Add the chicken, carrots, beans, cabbage, turnips and leeks. Season to taste. Simmer for another hour, add the sausage and potato and simmer for a third hour.

When everything is thoroughly cooked, strain off the stock and serve as a soup, topped with croûtons.

Carve the meat, which should be very tender, into slices and serve with the vegetables on a large platter as the main course.

◀ *The refined and tasteful world of M Gaudon's Chocolaterie Deleans in Rheims.*

amazing aromas of fresh chocolate.

Fresh, because all the chocolates are made by M Gaudon in the kitchen behind the shop. He proudly explains that he is one of a select group of *maître artisans* in chocolate, known as Le Club des Croquers, whose creations are sold exclusively in their own shops. You will have to go to Rheims to taste his *nélusko*, plain chocolate surrounding a cherry soaked in Cognac for three years; his pralines, almond-filled bites; or his *palets de café*, wafer-thin slivers of coffee-flavoured chocolate.

Over a small cup of bitter coffee – "the only drink to have with chocolate", he says (although I can recall meals in the French style, where champagne was served with coffee and chocolate) – M Gaudon talks about how to make the very best chocolate. First, find the best cocoa pods – he buys his from Central America and the Ivory Coast. Next, the pods need just the right amount of grilling – like coffee beans. The different chocolate grounds are then mixed until they have the perfect aroma: "Chocolate should be neither too sweet, nor too bitter. It should stay on the palate, leaving just a hint of bitterness, and very little sweetness."

But M Gaudon's story is bitter-sweet in itself. He is the last chocolatier in the département of Marne; he has no heirs and with him will go a tradition of small-scale artisan chocolate making. The people of Rheims will have to buy even greater quantities of factory-produced chocolate from the supermarkets and the shop will, I expect, simply be turned into a boutique.

On walking into Jean Aquatias' tiny charcuterie shop in the village of Ay near Epernay, you sense that here is a true family firm. His daughter is busy selling the award-winning black and white puddings and numerous *pâtés* and hams. Charcuterie plays an essential part in Champenois cuisine – pork being the region's staple meat. And in these kitchens, hams from Rheims are being mildly cured or smoked over broom cuttings. There are strong, mean little sausages, sometimes flavoured with local red wine, *andouillettes*, the classic pork sausages made from chitterlings – the best are reputed to come from Troyes, to the south – and bacon, usually sold unsliced, which is a regular

Salade de Cresson au Lard

WATERCRESS SALAD WITH BACON

This salad is made in a variety of forms throughout the region. The ingredients can include dandelion leaves, rocket or other salad greens, and garden herbs such as chives. Small, new potatoes (150g (5oz), boiled whole) can be substituted for mashed potato, if preferred. Croûtons and a poached or fried egg are sometimes added to make a very substantial dish. All in all, not so much a starter, more a meal in itself. A non-vintage champagne, perhaps one already served as an apéritif, would go well with this dish.

Serves: 4

Preparation time: 20 minutes

Cooking time: 40 minutes

300g (10oz) watercress

150g (5oz) potatoes, suitable for mashing and sautéing

150g (5oz) lean bacon

1 onion

1 shallot

5cl (2fl oz) wine vinegar

vegetable oil/lard for cooking

salt, pepper

Wash and drain the watercress, discarding any straggly stalks. Peel the potatoes, boil until soft and then mash. Chop the bacon into 1cm sq cubes and sauté gently in its own fat until well cooked but not too crisp.

Chop the onion and shallots finely. Place in a pan with a little oil (traditionally, lard is used) and the mashed potato. Heat gently until the oil is absorbed.

At the same time, in a separate pan, pour the vinegar over the bacon, bring it just to boiling point and then stir the bacon and vinegar into the onion and potato mixture. Season to taste with salt and pepper (taking care if the bacon is salty).

Finally, add the watercress and let it heat slightly until warmed through. If dandelions are used the same technique applies; if other salad leaves are used (lettuce for example), stir in but do not heat.

Serve at once, warm from the pan.

► *Jean Aquatias with his medal-winning black and white puddings, staple products of Champenois cuisine.*

feature of the region's salads (see recipes).

M Aquatias proposes some *pâté en croûte*, a local dish that traditionally puts in an appearance, hot from the oven, on Christmas Day, but is just as at home on a warm summer's day, eaten cold.

"But first we must cook it", I am told – and a fascinating exercise in speed and precision follows. Pastry is made in seconds, rolled out and put on one side while the *pâté* is prepared. Fillet of pork is chopped into cubes. Pepper, salt, local mustard from Meaux, parsley, a shallot and a little sugar are added before M Aquatias finds it necessary to open a bottle of champagne so that he can add a glass to the *pâté* mixture – and offer me one to drink. It is a *brut* champagne from the local cooperative at Ay – young and still quite green. He mixes fast, wrapping the *pâté* into a pastry parcel, coating it in egg to give a golden colour. Thin strips of pastry are cut out and spread on top for decoration, small slits are made for the steam to escape and into the oven it goes for 25 minutes at 200°C. The whole operation has taken just ten minutes. Mouthfuls of *pâté en croûte* are soon being washed down with just a little more of the local champagne.

More champagne at an unexpected, but welcome, time was forthcoming the next day when I visited Les Délices de la Ferme, the cheese shop belonging to Jacques and Renée Vautrin in the centre of Epernay. For me – as for many other visitors to Champagne – Epernay is a more accessible and charming town than Rheims, more closely linked with the wine culture and having one of the grandest wine streets in the world, the Avenue de Champagne, lined with the offices of a litany of major producers – Perrier Jouët, Mercier, Moët & Chandon – their cellars stretching out for dozens of miles below.

Inside is an enticing display – every imaginable cheese from all over France, and a few from beyond. The locals are making careful selections, being offered slivers to taste if they are unsure of a cheese's condition, discussing with Mme Vautrin whether a cheese is *à point* (ready to eat) or needs a few more days *élevage*, the omnibus term for the maturing or raising up of any kind of food or drink until it reaches its finest state.

Behind the scenes the atmosphere is more relaxed. Jacques Vautrin is not just the owner of a

◄ Pâté en croûte, *made in minutes by Jean Aquatias, and accompanied - why not? - with a glass of champagne.*

cheese shop, he is a "fromagophile", a lecturer on cheese at the local catering schools, a walking encyclopedia on the subject – and a devotee of a glass of champagne at midday.

Over a glass of soft, mature and creamy *brut* champagne, and surrounded by tasting samples, we discuss the local varieties. These include the *Cendré*, made at Baye in the Marne, a small, soft cows' milk cheese ripened and preserved with a covering of ash made from vine prunings, and traditionally made in the spring to use up a surplus of milk. Champagne is in fact less a cheese-producing region than one surrounded by such regions. From the town of Meaux, almost on the outskirts of Paris, comes the famous Brie de Meaux, probably the finest version of one of France's most celebrated cheeses (although those who prefer stronger cheeses swear by the Brie from Nangis). The milk used is drawn from a wide area, including Champagne, and throughout the Ardennes. In the Haute-Marne, to the southeast, the best-known cheese is Langres, from the birthplace of Diderot; a soft, yellow cheese with a depression in its centre, traditionally filled with *marc de Champagne* (the local brandy), which soaks in to give a rich smoothness. From the Aube comes the milk-white Chaource, a strong-tasting, very soft cheese which

Sabayon

While not strictly coming from Champagne, this dish sums up perfectly the essential lightheartedness of its sparkling wine. Sabayon is a version of Italy's zabaglione, *made with champagne rather than Marsala. If using quantities of expensive champagne in cooking is difficult to accept, substitute a Crémant de Bourgogne, Crémant d'Alsace or Saumur. However, at the Château de Saran, where this recipe originates, they naturally use the house champagne: Moët & Chandon.*

To drink: a light and fruity brut *non-vintage champagne, perhaps even a Blanc de Blancs.*

Serves: 6 people

Preparation time: 5–10 minutes

Cooking time: 5–10 minutes

6 egg yolks (size 2 eggs)

200g (7oz) caster sugar

quarter bottle *brut* champagne

Whisk the egg yolks and sugar together in a bowl until they have the consistency of thick cream. Place the bowl over a pan of simmering water, and whisk vigorously while adding the champagne. Continue to whisk until the mixture has doubled in volume and is very thick and fluffy. Remove from the heat and serve in tall glasses.

Sabayon can also be served chilled, topped with fruit; in which case draw the bain-marie from the heat and continue to beat the mixture until it is cool to preserve the light consistency.

▼ *A selection of local cheeses, including the shocking red Boulette d'Avesnes and sombre Cendré de Champagne.*

has been made in Champagne since the 14th century. To the north, there is the salt-washed Maroilles, while from further east there is Carré de l'Est, similar to Camembert, and Boulette d'Avesnes, a bright red, lethal-looking pyramid-shaped cheese (all pyramid-shaped cheeses seem to be particularly strong) flavoured with paprika and other spices – excellent in a French version of Welsh rarebit.

As we discuss – and nibble – these cheeses I am also speculating on their affinity to champagne. Brie certainly marries well, as does the local Cendré. Blue cheeses, M Vautrin tells me, go well with sweeter styles of champagne – with *demi-sec* or even *doux*, and with full-flavoured but dry rosés. With really strong, tangy varieties of cheese, however, you have to turn to a still Coteaux Champenois for accompaniment.

At the Restaurant Le Mesnil-sur-Oger, in the heart of the Côte des Blancs vineyards near Epernay, I tried some of the strong-tasting Langres with the famed – if only because of the name – Bouzy Rouge. This Pinot Noir-based wine is rarely heavy, but in good years, such as '88 or '89 it has the weight of a light red burgundy, and its inherent fresh, strawberry fruit flavours enhance the taste of the cheese splendidly.

These were by far the strongest tastes in a lunch which was more notable for the delicacy of its flavours. The chef, Claude Jaillant, is keen to promote this style of cuisine because, he believes, it marries best with champagne: "Champagne is a wine of life, of vivacity. I try to use local ingredients with plenty of taste and then create food that is light." True to his word, the *ris de veau* (calves' sweetbreads) are ever so lightly braised, and served with gently-flavoured Girolles mushrooms. The dish is lifted by a Blanc de Blancs champagne – the local wine – and the flavours never threaten to dominate the wine's very light, fresh character.

M Jaillant talked about the hierarchy in which champagnes should be drunk at a meal. Start with a non-vintage (best with fish, he believes), move on to vintage with the meat course, and then a rosé with the cheese – so progressing from lighter to heavier champagnes. It is an unusual succession of wines for a meal – one that would only be consumed in Champagne, and probably only with a champagne producer, but it can succeed. It's much

► *Le Vigneron's interior is a riot of* fin de siècle *posters for champagne and very large (empty) bottles.*

more likely that a Champenois would drink red wine with the meat – usually a Bordeaux, being more readily available (simply because more is made) and cheaper than burgundy.

But, at Le Vigneron, Hervé Liégent's restaurant in Rheims, I had sampled possibly the widest range of Champagne's own still wines that I am ever likely to drink. The restaurant is housed in a triangular room, the entrance at the apex. Coming in through this narrow way, you are confronted with a cross between a museum and a restaurant. On all sides are posters advertising champagne, many from the great age of champagne promotion at the turn of the century – except, that is, for one wall, along which stretches a ceiling-height glass-fronted case filled with every conceivable artefact used at one time for growing grapes or making champagne. With these is a series of tableaux depicting life in

▼ *Hervé Liégent and his chef Yannick Guichauoa outside Le Vigneron in Rheims: supporting Champenois cooking.*

CASTELLANE
EPERNAY
PREMIÈRE MARQUE
DE CE NOM
CHAMPAGNE
LOUIS ROEDERER
Champagne
POL MAUROY
DEUTZ

the region in the early 20th century.

From the realization that M Liégent is an enthusiastic promoter of his region, it is only a short step to understanding that he is the best advocate of its cooking – of a cuisine that is sometimes dismissed as colourless and poor. But put that description to him and he positively bristles with indignation – and with his chef, Yannick Guichauoa, he proceeds to put on a culinary display that completely justifies his loyalty.

We start with a glass of Blanc de Blancs as an apéritif, light and full of life. Somehow, however often it happens, I continue to approve of this way of starting a meal. But, from this point on, the region's red wines accompany four courses drawn from every corner of Champagne.

A red from the village of Les Riceys, in the Aube département, in the south of the region, accompanies the first two dishes. The village is better known for its Rosé des Riceys, but also produces tiny quantities of red from Pinot Noir grapes. The wine's natural acidity makes it light, and it goes well with a rabbit *roulade* (similar to a galantine) touched with walnut oil – a recipe typical of the Ardennes, a forested region full of game. Next, *feuilleté d'escargots de Dormans*, shelled snails from the village of Dormans in the Marne Valley, cooked in a puff pastry case and served with leeks and a *beurre blanc* made with champagne.

A change now to a heavier red, an '85 from Ambonnay on the Montagne de Reims, with *fricassée de volaille* cooked with *fine de la Marne*, brandy from the Marne Valley, which gives the chicken dish a kick of excitement and an opulent flavour. To this, the smooth, mature vanilla taste of the wine stands up well, but it is too soft for the last savoury course, a Chaource cheese cooked as a *gratinée*, which needs a return to the more acidic red wine from Les Riceys. Finally, *mille-feuille à la crème de pain d'épices* – the spicy cakes encountered at Biscuit Fossier – served with wild strawberries and ice cream; hardly a dish that the peasant women of Champagne (facing me, as models, from inside the glass cabinet) are ever likely to have eaten.

What this meal proves – and it's true of other dishes on the menu at Le Vigneron, like the impressive-sounding *andouillette de Troyes* with grilled bacon and a champagne vinegar sauce or the sander cooked in a sauce with pigs' trotters (called *pieds de porc de Sainte-Menehould*) – is that to be acceptable

▼ *Even in the heart of France, fresh shellfish is found every day at market.*

in an age when people demand lighter food, the region's classic dishes have had, on occasions, to be adapted. In their methods of preparation and blends of ingredients, they have had to move away from an era when they were cooked to provide ballast against cold winters, as well as sustenance.

And, as many of the region's cooks point out, their principal wine demands a lightness of touch that the traditional dishes cannot offer. This view, put first by M Jaillant, is reiterated by Jean-Claude Rampach of Le Caveau restaurant in Cumières, close to Epernay and right on the banks of the Marne. His Menu Surprise – you have no idea what you will be eating until the dish is placed in front of you! – has seven courses which owe more to the qualities associated with champagne than to the region's native cuisine. Grilled lobster, crayfish with truffle butter, a sorbet made with the local red Cumières wine, rabbit kidneys in red wine, fillet of beef with Girolles mushrooms, a salad with warm goats' cheese and a *gratinée* of red fruits is hardly traditional Champenois fare, but has plenty of quality local ingredients included for their own worth.

It can be seen that champagne is very much a locally appreciated wine and that the resourceful French have adapted dishes to suit it while remaining loyal to home-grown ingredients.

All this has happened in a region that has suffered so greatly from the upheavals of war over the centuries that the gradual development of any truly regional cuisine has been a battle in itself.

The dilemma of a traditional, staunchly rustic cuisine being out of tune with the times is very much evident in Champagne, but I certainly wouldn't want to see the traditional dishes disappear through neglect. When, on my last night, I essayed a local delicacy, *tête de veau* (calf's head) served with a caper sauce and cooked by its premier exponent, Mme Schoessler of La Touraine Champenoise at Tours-sur-Marne – out of retirement for the evening to prepare this dish – I was eating something that has its roots in peasant cooking. In her day as chef, devotees travelled from Paris to Tours-sur-Marne just for this one dish, a marvellous statement of solidity and good fare in a world that is rapidly forgetting such pleasures. Let us hope such rich, yet simple cooking, a style that has been refined over generations, does not disappear before the wheel of fashion turns full circle.

Râble de Lièvre Rôti et Champignons des Bois au Coteaux Blanc de Champagne

ROAST SADDLE OF HARE WITH WILD MUSHROOMS IN A SAUCE OF COTEAUX CHAMPENOIS

This recipe was given to me by Claude Jaillant, chef-proprietor of Restaurant Le Mesnil. The ingredients are all local to Champagne, but may not be readily available elsewhere, so I have suggested some alternatives.

The wine used in the cooking should be mature, with no aggressive acidity; a Chablis or light, unoaked Chardonnay could be substituted for the suggested white Coteaux Champenois. All three make suitable partners for drinking with this dish.

Serves: 8 people

Preparation time: 20–30 minutes

Cooking time: 50 minutes

4 saddles of hare, boned

65cl (22fl oz) chicken stock (or other light meat stock)

half bottle white Coteaux Champenois

6 basil sprigs, chopped finely

4 cooking apples

250g (9oz) potatoes

200g (7oz) wild mushrooms: Girolles(Chanterelles), Trompettes des Morts (Horn of Plenty) and Pieds de Mouton (Hedgehog Fungus) (or large Paris mushrooms)

100g (4oz) *foie gras* (or a smooth meat terrine)

vegetable oil for cooking

salt, pepper

Wash the saddles of hare, pat dry with absorbent paper and season with salt and pepper. Heat some oil in a deep frying pan and seal the meat, turning occasionally until brown all over. If you prefer meat a little less rare, cook the saddles for a few minutes longer. Remove from the pan and keep warm to one side.

Preheat the oven to 220°C (425°F, gas mark 7). Heat the stock and reduce to half the volume. Add the white wine and basil and simmer gently until the sauce is syrup-like. Remove from the heat and keep warm to one side.

While the sauce is simmering, core the apples and bake them in the oven for 20 minutes (they should still be firm when taken out of the oven). Peel and then slice them. Arrange the slices in the centre of a large serving dish, in the form of a rose.

Peel the potatoes, cut into chips and fry in a chip pan or frying pan. Heat some more oil in the frying pan and sauté the mushrooms. Keep the mushrooms and chips warm to one side.

Carve the hare saddles into slices, like small escalopes, and arrange around the apple, interspersed with small slices or spoonfuls of the *foie gras* (depending on its firmness). Finally, place the mushrooms and potatoes around the edge and pour the sauce over the meat.

WINES OF CHAMPAGNE

Champagne, more than any other wine, is an expression of both the place from which it comes and the way in which man has interpreted it. It is also one of the supreme articulations of our wine culture, a symbol of celebration and gracious living, and – it must be said – a fantastic marketing success.

Ironically, for a wine that has come to be synonymous with warm and festive feelings, it is the product of an inhospitable climate – Champagne, in northeastern France, is a cold, windswept part of the world. The low average temperature – a mere 10°C – means that these vines are living at the limit of the conditions necessary for their cultivation. Small wonder that the region's wine can be naturally tart and acid.

It can be drunk as a still wine, certainly – and there is a small market for Coteaux Champenois – but, with so many better wines to choose from, it remains a local curiosity. The wine has a tendency to re-ferment in bottle – and it was this characteristic that was used to advantage by the early pioneers of the champagne process as it evolved from the 17th century onwards. *Méthode champenoise*, in its final, perfected form, combines a wine with natural acidity with an ability to re-ferment in bottle to make a sparkling wine of unique character.

The vineyards of Champagne are conventionally divided into four main sections, with a smaller fifth section; some planting a mixture of the three grape types which make champagne, others specializing in just one.

The most northerly of these areas, lying on the northern slope of the Montagne de Reims, is planted with Pinot Noir – the classic red grape of Burgundy – producing fruity, full-bodied wines. A strip of vineyards winds its way around the hill and meets the second section, which runs westwards along the valley of the Marne, to the south of the Montagne. Here, the Pinot Noir is joined by the other red grape of champagne, the Pinot Meunier, whose wines are characterized by an earthy, gentle fruitiness, with less elegance and ability to age than the Pinot Noir. The third grape variety, the white Chardonnay, reigns supreme in the Côte des Blancs, a ridge of tree-topped hills stretching southeast from Epernay, and these wines have great liveliness, lightness and freshness.

The Aube, the fourth section, is some miles to the south, halfway to Dijon, and the smaller, fifth, concentration is around the hill-top town of Sézanne, between the Rivers Aube and Marne. These areas are planted with a mixture of all three varieties, but principally the two red grapes: Pinot Noir and Pinot Meunier.

Most champagne is a blend of two, or even three, of these grape varieties, each contributing something of their essential character. Some of the top wines will have 30 or 40 different constituents in the blend. The choice will be determined either by the master blender of a large champagne producer, or simply by the composition and location of a grower's vineyards, and great skill is employed in maintaining a house style.

A small quantity of wine will be made from just one variety – the light, often ethereal Blanc de Blancs from Chardonnay, or the rarer, rather heavy

▼ *Even an apartment block in Rheims can have links with the local wine, by playing host to unabashed advertising.*

▲ *The line that divides vineyards from fields in Champagne marks the northern limit of viticulture in France.*

Blanc de Noirs from Pinot Noir.

But by far the greatest amount of champagne is not only a blend of grapes, but also a blend of wines from different years. Non-vintage champagne aims to preserve a consistent character from year to year – so the style of a producer's wine is more important than the vintage. Because of this, champagne drinkers – like whisky drinkers – follow a particular, preferred brand, expecting that every time they ask for it, it will taste much the same.

However, in exceptional years, a small amount of vintage champagne is made, whose character is intended to be distinctive. Since this is made from some of the best wines of a good year, vintage champagne can be a great experience – although inevitably a more expensive one than non-vintage champagne. Up the scale from vintage – in price at least, if not always quality – are the so-called Cuvées de Prestige, made from the first pressing of the finest grapes and designed to be the absolute pinnacle of champagne, but often giving more in their packaging and promotion than in the experience. Both these styles, with their greater weight, are typically served with food in Champagne, while the non-vintage is usually drunk as an apéritif. At the end of a meal, the French enjoy a dry champagne, rather than a sweet wine – which, to the surprise of many outside France, the French often prefer to drink at the beginning.

Other varieties of champagne, apart from the Blanc de Blancs and Blanc de Noirs, are made in smaller quantities: Crémant is champagne made at a lower pressure than usual, but the term is gradually being phased out because of the confusion with sparkling wines from Alsace, Burgundy or the Loire. Pink or rosé champagne is a style usually made by adding a little red wine (from Pinot Noir grapes) to white champagne. Because of its extra weight and hint of tannin, it can be drunk with meat dishes or even with cheese.

All these champagnes have different degrees of sweetness, depending on the amount of sweetener added during the production process to soften the often searingly green character of the wine in its natural state. The driest of all, *sans dosage* (*dosage* is the term used for sweetening), has none added, and is something of an acquired taste. The next category, *brut*, is the standard dry style in which champagne most commonly appears. Moving up the scale, there are *sec*, *demi-sec*, *doux* and "rich", wines made only in small amounts and often for specific markets – sweet champagnes are popular in Brazil, for example. Though sweeter, these styles are never sweet enough to accompany desserts or fruit, but can be delicious with the light cakes and featherweight biscuits of the Champagne region.

Three different types of producer make champagne. Most familiar are the "houses", the great names of champagne which are widely seen, widely advertised and widely promoted – Bollinger, Krug, Veuve Clicquot-Ponsardin, Pol Roger. These are the firms that at the turn of the century created champagne's exclusive image, publicizing it as a drink for special occasions, for celebrating with – as a wine seen in the best company. While the "houses" may own vineyards, many of their grapes

► *The murals on the Hôtel de Ville (town hall) of Rheims celebrate aspects of the city's most famous industry, including basket-making for collecting the grapes, and cooperage.*

▲ *Flight of fancy at the Veuve Clicquot caves as the ancient gods celebrate champagne.*

◄ *Cellars carved out of chalk honeycomb the region, where millions of bottles ferment and mature.*

will also be bought from growers throughout the region who farm just small plots of land.

Some of these growers are now making their own champagne, which can be less expensive, but will also, inevitably, be a less complex blend, coming as it does from perhaps only one or two vineyards in just a single region of Champagne. And there is certainly greater inconsistency in small producers' champagnes, although the rewards for finding a good one can be great. The words Récoltant Manipulant or the initials RM appearing on the label identify a grower's champagne.

The third source is the cooperatives, who both make wine to supply the great "houses" and also bottle their own champagne – either under their own name or that of the retailer who is buying it. Cooperatives will never make the greatest champagne but they can make some of the best value.

Whatever style of champagne you drink, from whatever source, one thing is certain: that you will be drinking the greatest of celebratory wines. Its sophistication and festive nature may contrast with, rather than complement, the often rustic local cuisine, yet this wine's gently floating bubbles and exuberant froth, whether at the wedding breakfast or as the evening's apéritif, have firmly found their place in our society.

CHAMPAGNE

OTHER SPECIALITIES OF THE REGION AND WINES TO TRY WITH THEM

Champagne's turbulent past as a general battleground and thoroughfare for the rest of Europe has made it difficult for the region to build a broad-based, staunchly local cuisine. Yet homely dishes are plentiful, drawing upon river fish and forest game, as are more modern dishes, adapted to suit the qualities of champagne.

Soupe au boeuf des Ardennes originated in the wood-covered hills to the north of Champagne and is one of the warming soups, stews and *matelotes* (fish stews – the region has a special one, made with champagne) which are typical of the region, and intended to keep out the penetrating winter cold. In this one, cabbage – the region grows a profusion in red, white and green – swedes, leeks, carrots and potatoes are cooked with a nourishing beef stock, rather than with meat.

To drink: *a rosé champagne or red Coteaux Champenois, both with enough body and tannin to add to the warmth and richness of the soup.*

Pain à la reine is a smooth, light fish mousse made with pike and served with a crayfish *coulis*. This traditional dish from the banks of the Marne is rarely seen today but, making an attractive starter, it deserves a revival. The fish is puréed, bound together with *béchamel* sauce or *panada* (a flour mixture), cooked in a bain-marie and served hot. Meat *pains* are also made locally.

To drink: *the first choice for locals would be a non-vintage* brut *champagne, in a crisp, light style.*

▼ *Fish terrines in Epernay market – sophisticated dishes which even French cooks would buy rather than make.*

At one time, pike thronged Champagne's rivers – **brochet braisé au champagne** (pike braised in champagne) becoming one of the region's classic dishes. With its creamy sauce based on mushrooms, shallots and champagne, this is a lovely rich dish. Now that pike is rarer, salmon is sometimes substituted. Another recipe for pike – and now a standard French dish – is the delicate **quenelles de brochet**, poached pike mousse with a cream sauce.

To drink: *a* brut *or* Blanc de Blancs *non-vintage champagne, one that is light and crisp rather than too mature or rich.*

The game-rich Ardennes are still a source of wild boar – the emblem of the region. The meat can be pot roasted – **rôti de sanglier** – or casseroled with shallots, juniper berries, *lardons* and red wine (locally, a Bouzy Rouge) leaving the meat very tender. It is served sliced with simply-cooked root vegetables – turnips or swedes. The **marcassin ardennaise** casserole is made with young boar meat; *marcassin* being the term for a wild boar under six months old. At this stage the meat is still delicate and has not yet gained the very intense flavour of adult wild boar.

To drink: *a* Bouzy Rouge *from a good vintage, such as '89 or '90, which would have sufficient weight of fruit to counter the wine's natural acidity.*

▼ *The traditional* andouillette *incorporated in a light, modern dish.*

Champagne produces some of France's best charcuterie, making use not only of pork and mutton, but also of the region's game. Rabbit, hare and wild boar are turned into terrines, *pâtés, boudins* (black puddings), sausages and meat loaves. **Boudins de lapin** are sausage cakes based on rabbit, and there is **jambon de bête rousse**, wild boar ham.

To drink: *With these strong-tasting meats, try a rosé champagne or other pink sparkling wine. The rosé's extra body can cope with the powerful flavour of these meats.*

In this northerly area, root vegetables naturally feature widely in the cuisine. Potatoes are casseroled with onions and garlic, layered in a large pot and then baked in the oven, to make a dish called **bayenne**. Onions are also gently puréed with *marc de Champagne*. Dandelion leaves are cultivated for salads, to be topped with warm garnishes such as chicken livers, poached eggs and diced bacon.

To drink: *a white* Coteaux Champenois*, soft and light, with just a hint of the flavours of* Chablis.

Champagne's special method of preparation is called **à la Sainte-Menehould**, a term often applied to a dish of pigs' trotters, although other types of offal are used. The trotters or other meat are first cooked (for up to two days, until the bones are soft, in the case of the trotters) and then rolled in breadcrumbs and grilled. A piquant Sainte-Menehould sauce may be served too, made with mustard, vinegar, white wine, onions and herbs.

To drink: *a white wine such as the one used in the sauce, perhaps a* Coteaux Champenois

The people of Champagne have traditionally had a sweet tooth: tarts and pies filled with fruit in season – apples, blackcurrants, cherries and plums – are a favourite dessert, served with local cream. **Anglois** is a plum tart, its name being a reference to the red uniforms English soldiers once wore. **Gâteau mollet** is a raised sweet cake, similar to the Alsacien *kugelhopf*, and comes served with mousse or fresh fruit. Then there are waffles, crisp and dry or with a dollop of cream, and **brioches** – soft rolls or loaves made with a butter- and egg-enriched dough, and small iced honey cakes called **nonnettes**, a speciality of Champagne and Burgundy.

The **galette** has its origins in people's earliest experiments in cooking. These flat, round cakes have their basis in the cereal pastes made from wild or cultivated grain which were spread out evenly and baked as a staple food, thousands of years ago. Today, in Champagne, *galettes* made with cream and *brioche* dough are a favourite.

The simple fritter is found throughout France; Champagne's version, **beignets au fromage blanc**, is made with a soft cream cheese, formed into little balls, dipped in a light batter and deep-fried. Best served hot with a dusting of sugar.

To drink: *locally, a dry champagne would be served, providing a crisp counterpoint to the sweet food. For those who prefer a sweeter wine with desserts, try a* demi-sec *or even a* doux *champagne.*

PROVENCE

Of all the regions of France, Provence perhaps evokes the most emotional responses in north Europeans. For them, it is the land of sun, sea, olive trees and vines, the land of antiquities which goes back to the origins of western civilization. To the French, it is the resort for the *grandes vacances*, ruined perhaps by all those apartments, hotels and camp-sites, but still the place to relax and swim (in pools rather than the sea), to sail – and to be seen. For the gastronome, Provence has one of the healthiest cuisines in France, in which olive oil and garlic, herbs and salads marry with fish, simply-cooked meats and fresh cheeses, and where fruit so often substitutes for heavier pastries or desserts at the end of a meal.

With its refreshments, too, Provence has its own special contribution. *Pastis* – whether flavoured with aniseed or, more traditionally, with liquorice, is the apéritif of the true Provençal, and you will inevitably see men at café tables, glasses of cloudy white liquid to hand, carafes of water beside them for topping up. It's the drink for that magic hour in Provence: when the sun goes down, the smells of the land or the sea become more pronounced, and the glasses and bottles come out on a thousand patios. As for wine, there is rosé, in a dry, quite alcoholic style, often more orange than pink in colour, which, when well chilled, lends charm and pleasure to any Provençal meal. Its full, quite fat taste, sometimes lacking acidity, seems to blend with a range of foods, from shellfish to meat. And to complement the traditional rosé, there is an expanding range of reds and whites.

Provence is a vast region, stretching from the marshlands of the Camargue in the west to the Italian border in the east, bounded on the north by the Alps and on the south by the Mediterranean, which has always been the source of much of the region's food. Conquered and colonized since the time of the Phoenicians, today Provence is France's

▼ *Despite high property prices on the coast, inland Provence still has many secluded groves and hidden valleys.*

◄ *Sunflowers form an increasingly common crop in Provence, as elsewhere in France, and lend a warmth to the jagged mountain landscape typical of the region.*

▼ *Behind the glamour of hotels on the Côte d'Azur, towns still retain an almost medieval atmosphere.*

link with southern Europe. While most tourists arrive by plane or car, there is still the thrill, recorded by innumerable travellers in the thirties, of leaving the grey skies of Paris by overnight train and waking to the brilliant blue of a Provençal morning. For those who do drive down the A6 autoroute, there is that welcoming sign, somewhere north of Avignon, coinciding with the first olive trees: "vous êtes en Provence".

In fact to talk of Provence as a single region is almost impossible, so many different landscapes and climates are woven together into the whole. There is the Provence of the mountains, the secret, inland Provence, still rural and unspoilt in many areas, despite the regular influx of second-home owners and the establishment of older people retiring from the cold north. This is where the main vineyard areas are sited: the Côtes de Provence in the broad green valley of the Var, surrounded by barren mountains; the hinterland of Aix-en-Provence, that still unspoilt university town, producing top quality reds; and those of Les Alpilles, an area of fantastical mountains – like the surface of the moon – centred on the village of Les Baux-de-Provence.

In the east, there is the so-called Italian Provence, part of the kingdom of Savoy until the last century, an influence which remains much in evidence in its cooking – *pissaladière*, the traditional Niçoise version of pizza usually topped with sardines and anchovies, or *trouchia*, a blend of chard or spinach, herbs, cheese and beaten egg sold cold by the slice in grocers' shops in Nice. And not least there is that narrow strip of coast, hemmed in by the Alps, very similar in feel to its Italian counterpart: the French Riviera. Here is the Côte d'Azur, the original and still the smartest section of

Provence, forming a long, narrow strip of resorts that wind around the shoreline almost from the naval port of Toulon in the west right up to the Italian border. Abused, mocked, over-developed, it retains an aura and a style that come from its aristocratic origins and that set it apart from any of the more recently developed Spanish costas.

To most Provençaux, the coast is to be avoided: it is a foreign land to be visited perhaps in early spring when the almond trees are in blossom and the cafés on the Croisette at Cannes have tables to spare. Yet even in the biggest resorts like Cannes, life goes on behind the holiday-postcard scenes. Away from the grand hotels which stretch in an arc around the bay, there is the historic fishing port, still working, if only just. And there is the market, not simply meeting the needs of the many restaurants and hotels, but serving the locals who crowd in every morning to buy fresh from smallholders and fishermen.

I paid an early morning visit to the market in the company of Marc Berrut, chef-proprietor of

▼ *The waterfront at Saint-Tropez: for many people the most familiar image of the French Mediterranean.*

► *Street markets provide not only daily produce – this can be the conversational high spot of the day.*

La Cave, a restaurant in Boulevard de la République in the old part of Cannes. He specializes in Provençal cooking, using recipes his mother taught him. He is in fact one of a rare breed, a Cannois, with roots in the town going back six generations.

We walked behind the *mairie*, an imposing block of a building opposite the fishing port, and up the hill into the market. This is a true local market, with none of the *grossistes* – the wholesalers – who dominate the larger markets in France. Here, the fishermen are selling crabs, lobster and *rascasse* (scorpion fish), landed from their boats – now anchored a hundred metres away on the Quai Saint-Pierre – only an hour before. You see olives by the vat, fresh or dried, green or black, with mushrooms in olive oil, or with pine kernels. And there's a great Provençal delicacy, snails; stuffed with garlic and tomato they become *susarelle*.

Long before you see them, you smell the herbs of Provence: thyme, lavender, rosemary, sage, all fresh and enticing, bringing the smell of the fields into the kitchen. And just next to them are tiny courgettes, *fleurs de courgettes* which are flowers, or *courgettes en fleurs*, which are courgettes with their flowers on their ends. They are piled high alongside aubergines, that other essential Provençal vegetable, glistening purple-black – small ones for *ratatouille*, large ones for stuffing.

Then there's the fruit. Large red plum tomatoes, bright, ripe cherries and strawberries from the sun-baked hills behind the town, oranges and lemons from the groves that lie in the sheltered

▼ *Inviting and vivid: Provençal cuisine offers a fragrant reflection of its setting.*

Aubergines et Tomates au Gratin

GRATIN OF AUBERGINES AND TOMATOES

Aubergines and tomatoes are among the natural ingredients in a Provençal kitchen. They join red and green peppers, fennel, artichokes and green beans, all of which are used to make the finest light meals for the heat of summer. This simple vegetarian side-dish is easy to digest. As with many Provençal dishes, it should be sprinkled with a grating of hard cheese like Parmesan. Drink either the white wine used in the recipe, or a young, fresh, slightly chilled red, such as a Côtes de Provence.

Serves: 6 people

Preparation time: 15 minutes
(plus 30 minutes soaking time)

Cooking time: 1 hour

3 medium-sized aubergines
2 medium-sized onions, finely chopped
15cl (5fl oz) water
4 big, very ripe tomatoes (plum tomatoes are ideal, but not when tinned, because you need the skins)
1 large clove garlic, finely chopped
10cl (3½fl oz) dry white wine
1 tsp thyme, chopped
grated Parmesan cheese
olive oil for cooking
freshly ground black pepper
salt

Preheat the oven to 190°C (375°F, gas mark 5). Cut the aubergines into thick slices. Sprinkle them with salt and put aside for half an hour.

Rinse the slices, dry with kitchen paper and then fry them, in batches if necessary, in 4 tablespoons of olive oil, until they are almost golden.

Aubergines absorb copious amounts of oil, so you may need to add more oil to prevent them from sticking to the pan. Put the cooked slices to one side on more absorbent paper.

Add the chopped onions to the frying pan with 2 tablespoons of olive oil. Once the oil has been absorbed, add the water and leave the onions to cook slowly until puréed. Slice the tomatoes and grind a little black pepper over them. Pour a little more olive oil into a large shallow oven-proof dish, and alternate slices of tomato and aubergine until the base is covered.

Sprinkle the garlic over the slices, then add the white wine. Spread the onion purée over the top, and sprinkle with Parmesan cheese. Cook in the centre of a moderate oven for 30 minutes.

Serve this dish either hot or cold.

valleys behind the Côte d'Azur. Later in the year, there will be quinces, pears, apricots and peaches. There are the nuts – almonds mainly – which feature so frequently in Provençal meals, either as appetizers with *pastis* or as that special ingredient in tarts and flans (see recipes).

At half past eight in the morning, when the sunshine has still to find its way into some of the narrow alleys that wind through the old quarter of Cannes, this market is alive with housewives out shopping for lunch. This is a daily event; they all have their favourite stalls and much chaffing goes on as well as serious discussion – although the obvious enjoyment of everyone is never in doubt.

The short, sharp climb up the hill to the castle and the church is rewarded with a view of Cannes which shows how the resort area is simply an accretion to the old town. Settled in its bowl of hills, the town proper faces the heart of the bay and the islands of Lérins. The grand hotels seem

▼ *The olive and its oil, which is used to preserve vegetables and cheese, are the essence of the Mediterranean.*

▲ *The smell of lavender, grown for the perfume industry at Grasse, seems to fill the entire region.*

like mere appendages straggling out to the east, leaving the town to get on with its business.

I had met M Berrut the day before at what was described as a *journée provençale*, but which was really a get-together of restaurateurs from all over the Riviera in the vineyard setting of Domaines Ott's Clos Mireille near Hyères, a town easily missed for the number of bypasses surrounding it. Once past the inevitable hypermarkets the country becomes relatively unspoilt and the farm of Clos Mireille sits on the edge of a secluded hollow with a view of vineyards stretching away to the sea, and no other buildings in sight.

My host for the day was Olivier Ott, known around the world as an ambassador for his family's wines. After lunch, he was planning to speak to the replete restaurateurs about one of his favourite preoccupations, the matching of Provence wines with Provence food. As he told me: "It's time that

▼ *A charcutier may sell other local specialities: fish soup, Alpine lamb and, of course, wines to wash it all down.*

▲ *Herbs, dried onion, nuts and spices: the display brings to mind the markets of North Africa.*

we thought of wine as part of eating rather than as a thing in itself, that we thought of wine as a partner with food, not to be tasted in a vacuum, but at the table. Each region has wines which offer a close affinity with the food of that region. In Provence, our wines are for all occasions, not just for special ceremonies as with champagne. We have great combinations as well – fish from the rock pools, served with white wines, langoustines cooked with saffron and served with a typical, peppery rosé or the lamb from Sisteron with a red, a Coteaux d'Aix-en-Provence perhaps, or a Côtes de Provence." This I wanted to hear.

It was, however, a speech that was never made. The effects of lunch, under the trees, unaffected by a short, sharp downpour, were such that his

Tarte au Citron et aux Amandes

LEMON AND ALMOND TART

Lemons and almonds are grown widely in Provence, their harvests coinciding late in the year. Provençaux favour light and refreshing fruit-based dishes rather than complicated desserts, but there is a tradition, particularly inland, of tarts and pastries.

Serves: 6 people

Preparation time: 40 minutes (plus 1 hour resting time)

Cooking time: 45 minutes

For the pastry

- 2 eggs (size 2)
- 100g (4oz) sugar
- 200g (7oz) self-raising flour
- 125g (4½oz) unsalted butter
- pinch of salt

For the filling

- 3 eggs (size 2)
- 130g (5oz) caster sugar
- zest and juice of 1½–2 lemons, depending on size
- 130g (5oz) unsalted butter, softened
- 75g (3oz) ground almonds
- 25g (1oz) peeled almonds, halved
- lemon slices for decoration

In a large bowl, beat the eggs with the sugar and salt. Sieve in the flour gradually, beating all the time, to form a paste. Chop the butter into small cubes, and incorporate it into the paste by hand or using a blender. Shape the pastry into a ball and refrigerate for at least 1 hour.

Preheat the oven to 200°C (400°F, gas mark 6). Roll out the pastry thinly on a floured board to line a 30cm (12in) diameter flan dish. Work quickly to prevent the pastry becoming warm - if it does, return it to the refrigerator. Prick the pastry with a fork.

Cut a circle of greaseproof paper or aluminium foil to fit the base of the dish and put it over the pastry. Spread some china balls or dried lentils over the paper and cook the case blind in the centre of the oven for 15 minutes, so that the pastry case is dried, but not completely cooked. Remove the balls or lentils and the paper.

Reduce the oven temperature to 190°C (375°F, gas mark 5). Beat the eggs and sugar together until the mixture is light and fluffy. Add the lemon zest and juice, then the softened butter and ground almonds and mix thoroughly. Pour the mixture into the flan case, arrange the sliced almonds on top.

Cook the tart in the centre of the oven for 30 minutes, or until the filling is firm and golden brown.

When cool, decorate with slices of lemon.

audience's mind was on other things by the time the meal was over. It was a meal of great humour – a restaurateur likes nothing better than to have a good meal when he or she is not cooking.

We started with a cold buffet – a meal in itself in fact. The smoked salmon and melon were hardly local, but the ripe plum tomatoes, courgettes and onions were: all filled with a delicate stuffing of breadcrumbs, garlic and sausage meat, held together with a beaten egg and milk, and topped with melted cheese. Red peppers marinating in typical Provençal fashion in olive oil, slices of tuna, fresh from the Mediterranean and dressed in more oil, and gleaming black mussels in a white wine *bouillon* were piled onto plates. And to drink: white and rosé wines, the zingy fresh white going with the fish dishes, a crisp, light style of rosé with the stuffed vegetables and, as a bonus, with the salmon. Still more buffet appeared, accompanied by different,

▼ *Devil's kitchen: Provençal sausages, like the wild boar sausage in the foreground, tend to be hot and spicy.*

▼ *The morning's catch awaits the careful and critical scrutiny of local cooks anticipating a tasty* bouillabaise.

weightier rosés and some reds too. Mushroom and courgette fritters, smoked ham from the mountains of the Lubéron in the north of Provence, a salmon in a herb sauce. The salmon was the perfect partner for the rosé, the other dishes working equally well with either red or rosé.

We moved on to dishes for the richer red wines of Provence: Bandol, from the Ott estate of Château Romassan (although in another place we could equally well have drunk a Coteaux des Baux-de-Provence or a Coteaux d'Aix-en-Provence). The first was a simple meat dish, lamb from Sisteron, a mountain region close to Aix-en-Provence. The

► *Vegetables from market-gardens in the hills above the coast are brought into Cannes market daily.*

1 kg
1650
origine
produit
variété
calibre
1 kg
1350
VARIETE
ORIGINE
CATEGORIE
CALIBRE
AM

◄ *Eating* dehors *doesn't mean eating lightly, in France. This plate of Sisteron lamb is given the Provençal touch by the stuffed red pepper – and, of course, the backdrop.*

succulent meat, served with *ratatouille*, had a flavour that comes from the herbs which the lamb eats as part of its pastoral diet – thyme, savory, rosemary, marjoram and hyssop. Two styles of goats' milk cheese followed: one drier to partner white wine, the other light and fresher, to be enjoyed with red.

Then, speeches forgotten, it was time to relax. Some headed off for the seashore; others organized teams for *pétanques* in the courtyard. For me, a brisk walk through the vineyards, and it was time to head back to my hotel in Antibes, and a light *salade provençale* of mushrooms, red peppers, artichoke hearts, pork *rillettes* – a potted meat flavoured with herbs – a glass of rosé, and bed.

The next day I was bound for Cap Ferrat, a narrow promontory east of Nice jutting out into the sea to form the eastern end of the Bay of Naples – the Baie des Anges – green and wooded, the occasional villa among the trees, few cars, certainly no noisy motorcycles.

The route from Cannes to Cap Ferrat is by autoroute, high into the mountains behind Nice, through tunnels and across narrow valleys, where the suburbs of the city creep up the hillsides, filling seemingly impossible spaces. The few glimpses of the coast reveal hotels and large apartment blocks silhouetted against the blue sea and jostling for space in the hot and crowded conditions. It's all the more surprising, therefore, that so close to this is the paradise of Cap Ferrat.

My destination is the Hôtel Bel-Air, a former summer palace for the kings of the Belgians, white and glittering against the blue of the sky and sea, with immaculate gardens spreading out to the cliff edge, and a swimming pool in the rocks below. The last word in comfort, luxury and decadence certainly, where perfume advertisements are regularly shot, Hôtel Bel-Air is also home to the kitchen of a chef who is aiming to show how firmly his cooking is rooted in its Provençal origins.

Jean-Claude Guillon (a Burgundian, "but my heart is in Provence"), knows that however luxurious the hotel must strive to be, it is simplicity that

Tapenade

This is the classic dish that would be offered either in a restaurant or in the home in Provence as an appetizer. The quantity here is sufficient for a small party. The paste is spread on bread or toasts, or used as a dip with raw vegetables. It is also used as a stuffing for eggs (mixed together with the yolk of a hard-boiled egg). To accompany tapenade *a Provençal would either open a bottle of very chilled rosé or pour out a large* pastis.

Serves: 10–12 people

Preparation time: 5–10 minutes

50g (2oz) tinned anchovies
50g (2oz) tinned tuna
50g (2oz) capers
125g (4½oz) black olives, stoned
1 clove garlic
1 sprig thyme
1 bay-leaf
3 tbsp olive oil
freshly ground black pepper

Drain the anchovies, tuna and capers. Put all the ingredients except the olive oil and any seasoning into a blender and combine. Once the mixture is evenly blended, reduce the speed and add the olive oil slowly. Add a little black pepper according to taste (no salt will be needed). This paste will keep for several weeks in a fridge.

▲ **(Top)** *For centuries the technology has hardly changed – bread is still baked in this traditional oven every morning.*

▲ **(Centre)** *The baker's job remains one of the most vital in the community: if the local bakery closes, the village inevitably suffers.*

► *After shaping and proving the bread, M Collot spreads it out in the oven fan-wise to bake.*

► *The Hôtel Bel-Air at Cap Ferrat combines the glamour of the Cote d'Azur with a redefinition of Provençal cooking.*

imbues all the cooking of Provence, and that is what he is trying to marry with the grand style of the hotel. He talks of *michette*, the local bread brushed with olive oil; of garlic soup, served with bread in olive oil; of *pistou*, the local pesto paste made with pine kernels, garlic, olive oil and sometimes basil; of the black olives from the region around Nice; and of the fish which comes from the market of Monaco. True Provençal cooking, M Guillon believes, is one in which ingredients are simple and which derives from the comparative poverty of the land, so different from the lush north of France. That is why there are few cows here, why butter on the table comes from Normandy or from the Loire, and why some superb restaurants stay faithful to the olive oil and seafood tradition – and produce superb results.

The conversation turns to that most famous local meal, *salade niçoise*, a dish served and much abused around the world. It should, he says, be made from artichokes, green beans, black olives, spring onions, celery, sliced plum tomatoes, *mesclun* (a mixture of different young salad varieties

▼ *Fillets of red mullet with herbs and pistou butter, served on the terrace of the Hôtel Bel-Air.*

▲ *Jean-Claude Guillon, chef of the Hôtel Bel-Air, a Burgundian by birth - "but my heart's in Provence".*

and aromatic herbs) and should be dressed simply with olive oil and lemon juice.

And when he produces lunch, he is true to his word, and true to Provence in his choice of both food and wine. The rosé in traditional style, almost orange in colour, quite fat, seems to marry effortlessly with every dish – six courses in all. *Coquilles Saint-Jacques* come with asparagus tips and a basil and tomato sauce, *gâteau de homard* combines lobster and sole with chervil, vegetables, mayonnaise, breadcrumbs, with the essential Provençal garnish of olive oil, tomatoes and lemon juice.

This is followed by fillets of red mullet with herbs with *pistou* sauce, the fish floating lightly on the traditional Loire sauce of *beurre blanc*, but firmly anchored in Provence with the *pistou* (see recipes). And as a final fish dish, there is sea bream, served with leeks and potatoes, still light, even if not so truly Provençal. As if this isn't enough, the two sweets take advantage of local fruits and herbs in season: a tiny *gratinée* of wild strawberries – soft *crème brûlée* with the fruit beneath the crisp

Filets de Rouget aux Fines Herbes et au Pistou

FILLETS OF RED MULLET WITH HERBS AND PISTOU BUTTER

This recipe brings together a range of Provençal ingredients: red mullet, the herbs which are the essence of Provençal cooking, and pistou, *the Provençal version of the Genovese pesto (a jar of this can be used as a ready-made alternative). M Guillon uses pine kernels in his* pistou, *but Parmesan or Gorgonzola cheese are also popular. A crisp light white wine, such as a Cassis – or the Côtes de Ventoux used in the recipe – or equally a rosé Côtes de Provence would go well with this dish.*

Serves: 4 people

Preparation time: 20–25 minutes

Cooking time: 20 minutes

4 red mullet, each approximately 120g (4oz) (or 4 trout)

1 tbsp chopped fresh basil and chervil

1 tbsp white breadcrumbs

1cl (½fl oz) olive oil

For the pistou

1 clove garlic, finely chopped

6cl (2fl oz) olive oil

1 tbsp finely chopped basil

50g (2oz) pine kernels (or Parmesan/Gorgonzola cheese)

For the beurre blanc

50g (2oz) shallots, chopped

12cl (4fl oz) dry white wine (a white Côtes de Ventoux would be ideal)

6cl (2fl oz) cream

100g (4oz) butter

salt, pepper

Ask your fishmonger to fillet the fish. Clean the fillets. Set aside to dry on absorbent paper. Mix the fresh herbs with the breadcrumbs and a little of the olive oil to make a smooth paste. Re-shape the fish by taking two fillets and stuffing some of the paste mixture between them.

Make the *pistou* by mixing all the ingredients, using an electric grinder or by crushing finely in a pestle and mortar to make a paste. Set aside.

Preheat the oven to 190°C (375°F, gas mark 5). Prepare the *beurre blanc* by sweating the shallots in the white wine in a frying pan over a low heat. The liquid should reduce to the consistency of a thick sauce. Stir in the cream, reduce again over the low heat. Add the butter and stir until it melts. Season with salt and pepper.

In a non-stick frying pan, put a little olive oil and seal the fish parcels on both sides. Place in the oven centre for 5 minutes. At the last moment, mix the *pistou* with the *beurre blanc*, and spread around the fish.

Serve with potatoes and salad.

sugar top – and a plate of raspberries served with mint ice cream.

This is summer food, served against a backdrop of sun and sea. But inland, Provence doesn't bask in perpetual sunshine. The winters may be short, sometimes not setting in until after Christmas, but they can be intense, with harsh frosts, which can devastate the olive groves (as in 1985). But there can also be crisp, blue days, when there is something particularly magical about Provence. If the Mistral is not blowing, the air can be so still that the smoke from the chimneys just hangs in mid-air. It's a delicious smoke, from a mixture of vine and olive branches, a sweet smoke that promises good cooking rather than atmospheric pollution. For while most Provençaux will huddle inside their cafés, creating comforting fugs of smoke and alcohol, there will be those who, if they are not engaged in the annual hunt for the increasingly rare and expensive truffles, will march briskly into forests with their dogs to shoot whatever may be moving and bring it back for the pot.

The spoils of the weekend hunt form a major part of Provençal cooking in autumn and winter. Pigeons, pheasants, partridge, in fact any small game birds, are bagged, while rabbits, an ever popular ingredient, are frequently taken. Wild boar (*sanglier*) are still found in the mountains, although since I have never eaten any here, I am relying on hunters' tales. In Provence *sanglier* is simply cooked with the usual abundance of herbs, over a fire of vine cuttings, or in the oven, but, properly French, every other bit of the animal that can be used will be served: never forget this is a land where traditionally you ate what you could get.

After their exertions, the early morning hunters – who may be anything from bank clerks to farmers during the week – will consume glasses of rough, tannic red wine, ham or sausage (the *merguez* is prominent here, a bright orange-red sausage made of lamb and paprika, originating in North Africa, but now found in charcuteries throughout Provence), and vast quantities of bread thoroughly doused in olive oil and rubbed with garlic. After which, they will amble contentedly down to the café, the day's work done.

Even in the summer, game birds will still feature on menus – you don't question too closely what their origins are. For Gérard Chauvet, chef of the Byblos hotel in Saint-Tropez, pigeon was the logical culmination of a meal which had neatly combined a range of local traditions. We sat down to a tartare of finely chopped raw vegetables macerated in lemon juice, served with red mullet, this time in a sauce flavoured with truffles; a *pissaladière*, the octagonal pizza of Nice, topped with onions, tomatoes, black olives and anchovies; *courgettes en fleurs*, hollowed out and filled with mushrooms; sea bass served with fennel-filled ravioli topped with

Parmesan and fried lightly on one side. And finally the pigeon breasts, two each, cooked pink as is the custom in France, and served with Chinese cabbage filled with carrots and mushrooms.

Like my sumptuous lunch at the Hôtel Bel-Air, this was fairly grand cuisine. The night was warm, the swimming pool beside which we ate was still inviting, there was the sound of jazz from the club below. But we were again eating local ingredients, not drawing on international fare. And we were drinking local wines, a red Côtes de Provence of Château Barbeyrolles 1988, perfumed rather than heavy, and the richer, more spicy Château Minuty 1990, both from vineyards in the peninsula of Saint-Tropez. Provence, the international playground of the rich, has not forgotten its roots.

▼ *Geraniums, fading yellow walls and window shutters: the epitome of tranquillity in a small Provence village.*

WINES OF PROVENCE

Sun, sea and sand. This is the image of Provence that's transferred from the landscape into the wines. We perceive them as being young and jolly numbers, little more. No seriousness here.

For the vast majority of Provence wines this may be true. But there is a fascinating and growing minority to consider. A committed group of wine producers is taking advantage of the Mediterranean climate to create exciting, serious red wines which represent the future of Provence. And there are now producers making crisp whites which would have been impossible even 10 years ago, before the arrival of modern equipment in the cellars.

The place of Provence in French viticultural history is seminal. It was from here the vine travelled northwards up the Rhône Valley and so on into the rest of France. During the 6th century BC the Greeks founded the port of Marseilles and introduced their vines – and wine has been produced in Provence ever since. True, there are some traditions that owe their continuation more to their history than their current value. And there are some tiny historic appellations which only just survive. But its long association with the vine means that in Provence making wine is more embedded in the fabric of society and that drinking wine is more a normal part of Provençal life than in any other area of France.

Vineyards are found all over Provence. There are wines produced from the Italian border to Marseilles and from the hills of the Ventoux to the coast at Saint-Tropez. But there are two big concentrations. The first is the largest of the appellations contrôlées, Côtes de Provence. It forms an arc from Toulon, the great French naval base, sweeping northeast behind the Massif des Maures which follows the coast, to the resorts of Fréjus and Saint-Raphaël. The other, more compact, is west of Côtes de Provence, centring on the town of Aix-en-Provence. There is another smaller concentration on the coast between Marseilles and Toulon, where vines fight with villas for space around the holiday town of Bandol and Cassis, a small port.

The traditional wine of Provence is pink, strong and dry – and it can be quite dull. It is still the main

◄ *Traditional bush planting contrasts with more modern wire-trained vines as Provence transforms its wine industry.*

production of the appellation Côtes de Provence. The curiously tall skittle-shaped bottles are familiar sights on restaurant tables the length and breadth of the Côte d'Azur. The wines suffer from high prices, because of local demand from easy-to-please tourists, and an unfashionable colour: in many countries, pink wines are notoriously difficult to sell. Made from the Grenache and Carignan grapes, Provence rosés can be high in alcohol and low in freshness, although more modern producers are blending in some of the better quality Mourvèdre grape and, by using modern winemaking techniques which keep more of the fruit flavour, they are able to make some pleasantly drinkable wines with which to partner the classic salad and fish dishes of Provence.

The heat that makes rosés tend to high alcohol, and the whites tend to flabbiness does wonders for the reds of the Côtes de Provence. Growers are now concentrating on these, and are planting increasing quantities of more noble varieties – Mourvèdre, Syrah, even Cabernet Sauvignon – as they work hard to improve the quality-rating of Provence wines.

Smaller quantities of whites are made, and these, like the rosés, are benefiting from new winemaking techniques and equipment to keep their fruit flavour and freshness. The local white grape varieties are Ugni Blanc and Rolle; now Chardonnay, the staple white grape from Burgundy, and Sémillon from Bordeaux are giving an extra richness and flavour to the wines.

While the Côtes de Provence appellation produces by far the largest quantity of wines in Provence, it is the smaller areas that are making the very finest wines. The district around Aix-en-Provence is one of these. There are two appellations here: Coteaux d'Aix-en-Provence is the larger of the two. Its vineyards occupy a considerable area between the town itself and the Durance River to the north and a smaller section around the western side of the Etang des Pierres. Further west is the much smaller appellation of Coteaux des Baux-de-Provence, a flat, arid plain encased in a spectacular circle of rock outcrops.

A number of estates in both appellations – but

particularly in Les Baux where the vineyards are among the hottest and driest in France – are now producing very fine reds. In some cases they are taking advantage of the dry climate to practise organic vineyard techniques. Some producers – Domaine de Trévallon in Les Baux or Château Vignelaure in Coteaux d'Aix-en-Provence – are using 60 percent Cabernet Sauvignon in their blend along with Syrah, while other producers are trying Cabernet Sauvignon along with Syrah and Mourvèdre as foils to the more traditional local varieties, Grenache and Cinsaut. The result is wines of great elegance, a meeting of Bordeaux and the south in one bottle, the blackcurrant of a Bordeaux blending with the wild thyme aromas and rich, silky texture of a Mediterranean wine. These are the wines to drink with local lamb from Sisteron, or game from the Lubéron mountains.

Mourvèdre has a starring role in the appellation of Bandol west of Toulon. The red wines must contain at least 50 percent Mourvèdre, which may be blended with Syrah, Grenache, Cinsaut and Carignan. Bandol reds are big wines, sturdy and able to live long: their herb and truffle tastes are typically Provençal, but they manage an extra degree of style and quality that often eludes other wines from the region. Rosés are also made in Bandol – sturdier than those of Côtes de Provence.

Although the regions of Coteaux d'Aix, Les Baux and Bandol are undeniably producing the top quality wines and Côtes de Provence wins easily in terms of quantity, there are also some tiny appellations which survive through the efforts of a handful of producers, as well as the creation of two newer

▼ *The Baux-de-Provence vineyards, overlooked by their medieval village, give some of Provence's most exciting red wines.*

VDQS appellations. Palette is a two-producer appellation, dominated by Château Simone, whose red and rosé wines are made from Grenache, Mourvèdre and Cinsaut. The reds are serious, slightly old-fashioned, with spicy, oaky flavours, the rosés can be somewhat clumsy. And there is some white wine, which is also aged in wood.

The small white wine appellation of Cassis – not to be confused with the blackcurrant liqueur from Burgundy – produces aromatic and spicy wines, usually consumed with local seafood dishes, such as *bouillabaisse*, from the port which lends its name to the appellation. Similarly little is known, outside the locality, of the light, fresh whites of Bellet, from the hills inland from Nice. Red and rosé are also produced, but the white is generally the best – these are not great wines, but they do seem just right on a hot day on the Promenade des Anglais.

The newer VDQS appellations of Coteaux Varois and Coteaux de Pierrevert are still very much influenced by older attitudes towards the wines, emphasizing wood overtones at the expense of fruit flavours. Coteaux Varois, dominated by the cooperatives, also has a few private estates where, with the arrival of modern winemaking techniques and increasing use of Cabernet Sauvignon in the blend, some serious reds, similar in style to Coteaux d'Aix-en-Provence, are being made. Coteaux de Pierrevert shows signs of producing wines which are going to be simply quaffable, with few pretensions.

The main appellations of Provence will always be highly priced, simply because there is such a strong local demand. So it is to these newer areas in Provence that consumers away from the south of France are turning for value for money, and for some of the more exciting tastes from France's oldest wine region.

PROVENCE

OTHER SPECIALITIES OF THE REGION AND WINES TO TRY WITH THEM

The food of Provence is the quintessential Mediterranean cuisine. It combines simple, flavoursome ingredients from the sea and the land with straightforward cooking based on the use of olive oil. In an age concerned with balanced eating this is, for many, the healthiest cuisine in France.

Soupe au pistou offers a substantial mix of vegetables – carrots, French beans, haricot beans and courgettes – filled out with macaroni (revealing the Italian influence on Provençal cuisine) and flavoured with **pistou**, the local garlic and basil paste. In winter, dried beans, root vegetables and pumpkin are used.

To drink: *perhaps a fragrant, perfumed rosé from Bandol, a fuller, weighty one from the Côtes de Provence or a light, fresh, gently acid one from the Coteaux Varois.*

Pissaladière has its origins in Nice. The flan has a shortcrust pastry or bread dough base with a lip to hold the filling. It is spread with slivers of gently fried onion, just caramelized, and then sprinkled with anchovy fillets and black niçoise olives, for piquancy. Great simply to "cut at".

To drink: *any rosé from the region, crisply chilled – the more alcoholic style of Côtes de Provence would be ideal.*

Bouillabaisse is one of a number of fish stews, for which Provence has a passion. It originated in Marseilles, where fishermen returning with bursting nets cooked it there and then on the beach. But its invention has also been ascribed to divine inspiration: the goddess Venus is said to have created it for her husband Vulcan.

The more fish it contains, the better: conger eel, scorpion fish, cod, sea bass, flounder and shellfish are regular participants. Before being stewed, the firm-fleshed fish and shellfish are marinated with the most important elements of Provençal cuisine (ingredients that have given their name to the culinary term **à la Provençale**): olive oil, tomatoes, onions, garlic and herbs. Fennel, saffron and a slice of dried orange rind are also added. The soup and fish are served separately – the liquid soaked up by chunks of home-made bread.

To drink: *a light, fresh, crisp wine such as Cassis, a chunky Bellet, or a full-bodied rosé, such as a Côtes de Provence would be suitable.*

Cousin to *bouillabaisse* is **bourride**, a stew made with white fish only. At the end of the cooking, the stock is mixed with **aïoli** – a garlic mayonnaise – and poured over the fish.

To drink: *a crisply scented Cassis or a modern style of white such as those from the new estates of the Côtes du Lubéron.*

Rouille is a second enriching garnish used with fish. This potent, hot chilli pepper and garlic mayonnaise – whose name means "rust" – is often used to flavour the thick and creamy **soupe aux poissons**, a puréed fish soup.

▼ *Rabbit with garlic and rosemary and (top)* pieds et paquets.

Meat takes second place to fish in much of Provence, but, inland, meat stews such as **salmis**, usually made with woodcock, wild duck, pigeon or pheasant, have long been a favourite.

To drink: *a meaty, herby red Côtes de Provence, full of flavour to match the richness of the stew. This is also suitable for the rabbit dish pictured above.*

The traditional **pieds et paquets** consists of sheep's trotters with parcels of stuffed sheep's tripe, cooked in white wine.

To drink: *a quaffing red, such as a Vin de Pays des Bouches-du-Rhône, or a Coteaux Varois, perhaps.*

Gigot de broutard (leg of lamb) uses the succulent lamb from Sisteron, The meat, flavoured with the lavender on which the lamb grazed, is roasted, seasoned with thyme and rosemary, and rubbed generously with garlic – which can be added to a cream sauce.

To drink: *a full red Bandol, with the taste of truffles and herbs, or perhaps a Coteaux d'Aix-en-Provence or Coteaux des Baux-de-Provence, which both hint at the elegance of Cabernet Sauvignon.*

Excellent **estouffade** or daube of beef is made in Provence – the meat braised very, very slowly with white wine until extremely tender.

To drink: *any of the region's red wines, although a fuller style, such as a Bandol, would be ideal.*

Peppers, plum tomatoes, artichokes and aubergines become **tian** (*gratin*) – a special potato version comes from Apt, for which potato and chopped onion are layered, covered with grated cheese and laced on top with olive oil. And, of course, there is **ratatouille**: vegetables simmered with herbs to form a flavoursome ragout.

To drink: *a rosé would go well with these dishes, especially the more powerful, alcoholic Côtes de Provence.*

▼ Salade niçoise, *a much-abused dish, but still one of the great combination salads of Provence.*

Salade niçoise exhibits perfectly how Provençal cuisine can draw on locally-grown, fresh ingredients: artichokes, French beans, spring onions, celery, plum tomatoes, salad leaves and black olives – olive oil and lemon juice provide the simplest of adornments, but green peppers, hard-boiled eggs and anchovy fillets can be added.

To drink: *if eaten as a separate dish, try a white wine – a modern Côtes de Provence with a good dash of acidity.*

As with vegetables, so Provence burgeons with fruit: almonds often flavour pastries, wild strawberries are eaten with a touch of lemon juice or a taste of red wine; there are melons from Cavaillon, and juicy figs, peaches and nectarines.

To drink: *although Provence does not produce any sweet dessert wines, the richly sweet Muscats from Beaumes-de-Venise are close enough to be suitable.*

Some fruits are crystallized and, of these, a few become **calissons**: small, diamond-shaped cakes. A mixture including crystallized melon and orange, and blanched almonds is put on an unleavened bread base and iced. They date as far back as the seventeenth century, when they were given out at ceremonies held in remembrance of the plague. The cakes are best eaten when fresh and moist.

THE

LOIRE

VALLEY

Of the seven wine regions in this book, the Loire Valley is the least homogeneous. During the 1,000-kilometre course from its source high in the Massif Central to the Atlantic coast, France's longest river passes from high mountain country to lush meadows and orchards flanked by willow trees, through vineyards and on to the flat marshland, the *marais*. It goes through tiny villages, as remote as anywhere in France, and sweeps round historic old towns and numerous châteaux. During its course its character changes from an exhilarating mountain torrent to a wide majestic flow tending to flood. The river is joined by many tributaries but divided into channels by numerous islands and sandbanks, revealed during the summer months, which make navigation of this winding route impossible for any sizeable vessel.

What is true for the landscape is also true for the gastronomy of the Loire: there is very little link between the solidly meat-based cuisine of the Morvan and Forez regions of the Massif Central (the Auvergne is particularly famous for its smoked hams and sausage), and the seafood and fish caught off the Brittany coast at the mouth of the river. So it is with the wines: in the upper reaches of the river the firm, tannic reds have more in common with burgundy and Beaujolais than elsewhere while, at the estuary, white wines, affected by the proximity of the ocean, are crisp and tangy. Between the two extremes there is a wealth of choice; in all some 80 appellations belong to the Loire Valley, in a range of styles. Everything from the driest to the sweetest white, from light to some surprisingly heavy reds, as well as rosés and sparkling wines is produced along the sinuous length of this valley.

And yet there are connections. The wines – even the reds – are characterized by a lightness that comes from grapes grown and ripened in the comparatively cool climate of the northern half of France. And the region's food – the profusion of fresh, local fruit and vegetables, river fish such as sander (sometimes called pike-perch), eel, pike and crayfish, and meat, especially pork and beef – all go to make up a cuisine that is almost archetypically French, but which again points to the northerly location, for this is a land dominated by butter and cream, not by the olive oil and herbs essential to the south of France.

It comes as no surprise, perhaps, that in the 16th century the Loire Valley was home to Catherine de Medici. She is generally credited with having introduced Italian cooking to France, so

▼ *A typical Loire Valley riverscape: shallow waters and villages lining the riverbank beneath tufa cliffs.*

laying the groundwork for French cuisine as it is today. Not only in terms of food is the Loire Valley, to outsiders, the true France. The very name conjures up images of tranquil countryside, swathes of forest, small riverside towns, and fairy-tale châteaux in dramatic settings. Those who know the region talk of the quality of the light, gentle dappled light, that is associated more with Impressionist paintings than with classical landscapes – a soft, rich land with plump cattle and plump people.

These images derive from the stretch of the river beginning at Orléans – where the Loire is at its closest to Paris – and continues through the provinces of Orléanais, Touraine and Anjou and to the Pays Nantais, Muscadet country, at the mouth of the river. Here is the heart of France. The city of Tours vies with Poitiers as home of the best spoken French – certainly it is a region where it is easy for visitors to understand and be understood. For long the Loire was the hunting ground of French kings; it was here that they built their hunting lodges and, later, their castles. This France felt more like a home for royalty than an often hostile Paris.

The Loire and its tributaries – the Loir in Anjou, the Cher, Indre and Vienne in Touraine – form a visible barrier between the north and the south, between the flatlands of Picardy and the Ile de France and the great mountains to the south, from which the Loire descends. Other differences are noticeable too; the slate roofs of the north give way to the red pantiled roofs of the south, the work ethic of northern France opposes the two-hour midday *sieste* of the south.

Nowhere is this division more apparent than in the Pays Nantais itself. Within five minutes you can cross the river at Nantes and go from slate roofs in the city to pantiled roofs in the villages in the Muscadet vineyards, with their gaily-coloured shutters and Italianate air. While that feeling is literally present in the case of the small town of Clisson, designed to mirror a Tuscan hill village, it is to be found anywhere in the region, whether in the pretty, pedestrianized village of La Haye-Fouassière, home to the Maison des Vins, or in the altogether more substantial town of Vallet, dominated, like anywhere in the Pays Nantais, by the high nave and spire of its church.

Yet the Pays Nantais is curiously ambivalent. In one respect it looks south, in another it looks west, to Brittany. Muscadet and its foil, Gros Plant, are both wines that are drunk widely in Brittany – perfect partners for the seafood and fish which dominate the cuisine of the region. Nantes was the home of the Dukes of Brittany, an independent country until Anne, the last Duchess, became Queen of France, and her castle is still firmly in evidence in the centre of the city – a city which is generally thought of as being industrial, but which is surprisingly beautiful. Drive a few kilometres west of Nantes and the landscape changes completely out of the rolling vineyards of Muscadet into a land of marshes and stunted trees, with the salt-tang smell of the Atlantic Ocean in the air.

▲ *Despite Chinon's reputation for producing good red wines, the slate roofs show that this is still northern France.*

The regional park of Brière is part of the Celtic western fringes of Europe. To the English, this is Cornwall or Devon on the continent, complete with thatched cottages and narrow twisting lanes. One village, Kerminet (note the "Ker" prefix, which in Breton means "the home of" and which crops up all over Brittany), has been turned into a museum. But this being France, it also boasts an excellent restaurant, the Auberge de Kerminet. Yves Pebey, chef at the Auberge, produces a series

▲ *The cream of the nation: the Loire Valley supplies not only its own cooks with dairy products, but also much of France.*

of fish and fowl dishes which derive from the surrounding marsh and river area rather than the ocean: eels, frogs' legs, and *poisson du marais* (the local name for the sander or pike-perch, the fish that occurs throughout the Loire Valley). And there are pheasant and woodcock, and wild duck from the Lac de Grand-Lieu, a nature reserve to the south of Nantes.

The very homely nature of cooking in the region, relying on local ingredients, is nowhere better illustrated than by the contrast between the Auberge de Kerminet and the Hotel l'Océan on the coast at Le Croisic, a few kilometres away. Here, while watching the ocean breakers beating on the rocks outside the restaurant, you dine on the harvest of the sea: the land and river food of Kerminet could be an eternity away. We eat a *plateau de fruits de mer*: crab, langoustines, oysters and clams. I learn from my host, Jean-Paul Dorie of the area's tourist board, the local way of eating crab; ignoring the elaborate surgical instruments delicately laid out by the waiter, he produces a penknife, cuts the half crab in two, peels away the outer shell and proceeds to eat it rather like a baguette, holding it in his hands. It may not be elegant, but it works so much better. Easy eating is pleasant too.

Two wines accompany our ocean feast. First there is Gros Plant, the highly acidic white wine produced in small quantities in the Muscadet vineyards. The green taste and extra crispness give it the edge over a Muscadet when served with shellfish. Then we move on to a Muscadet de Sèvre-et-Maine *sur lie*, from the classic vineyard area between the rivers Sèvre-Nantaise and Maine south of Nantes. The wine has been bottled straight off its lees (*lie*), the yeast sediment which gives the wine extra flavour and freshness. By this time, the debris of shellfish has been cleared away and a procession of waiters has brought out what looks to be a mountain of salt on a huge platter. Cutting through this salt with a few deft movements, the head waiter reveals a sea bass, sealed whole in a blanket of salt to keep in its juices during cooking, its flavour just subtly enhanced by lavender and herbs from Provence. White and moist, not at all salty, it melts in the mouth, perfectly paired with the full, soft flavour of our Muscadet.

Apart from Muscadet, one other element of our

meal is always found with fish in the Pays Nantais: *beurre blanc*. This sauce, made with the local butter which is said to be among the finest in France, is made piquant by the addition of shallots and Muscadet (see recipes). Occasionally there are variations, chives (*ciboulette*) or parsley (*persil*) may be added, but in the Loire Valley wherever you find fish you find *beurre blanc*, and, thankfully, the recent controversial antagonism to butter has made no headway here – perhaps because the Loire is so close to that most resolute of dairy countries, Normandy.

On the north side of the Loire estuary the coast turns towards the Brittany peninsula and is known as the Côte Blanche, the white coast. It certainly sparkles as the sun hits the waves, but the rocks look grey. So, I ask, why white?

It's because of the salt, I am told, the salt that comes from the pans just north of Le Croisic, a promontory west of Saint-Nazaire. The very finest had covered the sea bass at lunch. I drove out to the middle of the *marais*, the marshland, a desolate landscape which seems to disappear without break into the sea. The salt pans look grey and un-inviting as the sun sulks behind a cloud. Mountains of salt are being shifted about in desultory fashion by a JCB. The salt of Guérande, the nearby fortified town, was sought after for many centuries, but with the development of the great salt pans of the south of France (the bulk is distributed by the Salins du Midi company which has a near monopoly on salt in France), and the ease of transporting it throughout the country, the existence of the *paludiers*, the salt producers at the mouth of the Loire, was in doubt. Only in the past few years, with the development of a cooperative, have things looked up. There's now a small museum, and salt is for sale in small packets.

There are three categories of salt – the whiter the better. The very finest is the *fleur du sel*, which comes from the top of the pan and is creamed off the *sel gris*, the grey layers, underneath. For a long time I eked out the packet of *fleur du sel* I bought at Guérande, as it has a freshness of ocean spray quite unlike the commercial product.

There's another taste of Brittany to sample here: the crêpes and *galettes*, those pancakes which are sold all over Brittany, filled with anything, say cheese or shellfish and which always provide relief

Rognons de Veau au Muscadet

CALVES' KIDNEYS WITH MUSCADET

This dish from Brittany is a reminder of the Pays Nantais' close links with Celtic traditions. In some parts of Brittany, cider would be substituted for Muscadet, but Bretons always include Calvados, the apple brandy of Normandy. Lambs' kidneys can be exchanged for calves' kidneys, if preferred. Either the Muscadet used in the recipe, a light, fruity red such as a Gamay from Ancenis or Touraine, or a dry Rosé de Loire, would be a good accompaniment.

Serves: 4 people

Preparation time: 20 minutes

Cooking time: 20–25 minutes

250g (9oz) streaky bacon (or ham)

200g (7oz) small onions

4 cloves garlic

12 calves' kidneys (or 16 lambs' kidneys)

20cl (7fl oz) Muscadet

1 tbsp Calvados (or Armagnac)

100g (4oz) unsalted butter

2 tbsp vegetable/sunflower oil
(or butter or calves' kidney fat)

salt, pepper

If the bacon (or ham) is salty, blanch it first: place in a pan of water, bring to the boil and cook gently for a few minutes. Dice when cooled.

Peel the onions, but leave the garlic unpeeled.

If there is any fat with the kidneys, remove this and put on one side. Take off the thin membrane covering the kidneys and any sinews inside. Chop the kidneys into 1cm cubes.

Melt half the oil in a thick-bottomed frying pan and, with the heat high, brown the kidneys quickly all over. Reduce the heat and cook for 6–8 minutes, making sure the interiors of the kidneys stay pink. Drain the kidneys from the pan and keep warm on one side in a serving dish.

Melt the rest of the oil or butter in the frying pan, add the bacon, onions and garlic and cook for 5–6 minutes, stirring occasionally. Stir in the Muscadet and Calvados and cook on a medium heat until the sauce is syrupy.

Season with salt and pepper, draw off the heat and blend in the butter. Adjust the seasoning and pour the sauce over the kidneys.

for frazzled parents puzzling over what to give their children to eat. It's in Nantes, though, that you find the man reputed to be the best pancake-maker in France. M Hoyet, who owns La Baguette *crêperie* hard by the Talensac market in the centre of the city, certainly supplies some famous addresses, including the Elysée Palace and the Hôtel Matignon in Paris, official residences of the President and Prime Minister of France. M Hoyet sends to Paris his vanilla-flavoured *crêpes dentelles*, paper-thin rolls of pancake, crisp and sweet, which are served as *gourmandises* at the end of a meal with coffee, so light and airy that it's perfectly possible to eat two or three without noticing amounts.

His sweet and savoury pancakes – *galettes* – are certainly something very special, too. I indulged myself in two of the house specialities, *galette La Baguette*, which is filled with tomato and herb-flavoured beef (washed down with a small pitcher of bone-dry cider), followed by a crêpe oozing with chocolate. My corner afforded a good view of the restaurant, itself a work of art, full of tinted photographs of ancient goings-on in Breton costume. The waiter and waitress, too, are dressed in traditional dress. The lilting sound of Celtic music completed the atmosphere.

The next day brought me back into the mainstream of French cooking, with a visit to the huge Marché du Min in Nantes, one of a small group of regional centres from which smaller markets are supplied, acting in much the same way as the Paris market of Rungis. The market is dominated by wholesalers and large suppliers but there is still room for the local chef and it was with Gérard Ryngel, chef-proprietor of Villa Mon Rêve at Basse-Goulaine just outside Nantes, that I arrived at five in the morning for the opening of the fish market.

This is a fascinating exercise in speed – lasting

for only one hour because to keep the fish fresh it has to be on the move as fast as possible – and, apparently, also in the ability to shout as loud as possible. In fact it seems more of a game for the stallholders, conducted with huge grins as somebody shouts over your shoulder or throws boxes of fish across an open space.

From M Ryngel I learnt a few tricks of the trade about buying fish. It's the eyes that count: they should be clear, staring at you, not cloudy and yellow. Pick up the fish and the tail should flip up. It should glisten with moisture rather than be too dry. And it should not smell fishy. So, with much gazing into eyes, flipping of tails and smelling of the fish, we bought sander for the lunch M Ryngel was going to cook for me (see recipes), as well as lobster (still alive, naturally), langoustines and eels.

But before that lunch, a brief tour around some of the food shops of Nantes introduced me to a

◄ *The Loire Valley is still a land of smallholdings, many hardly keeping their owners in a living.*

Croustillon de Sandre au Beurre de Muscadet

FILO PASTRY CASES OF SANDER IN A WHITE WINE SAUCE

This spectacular dish was cooked by Gérard Ryngel, chef-proprietor of the Villa Mon Rêve restaurant, just outside Nantes. Although sander, or pike-perch, the most familiar of Loire fish, is sometimes found in fishmongers' shops outside France, it is still rare and any freshwater fish with firm flesh – pike, trout fillets or salmon, for example – can be substituted. Drink a crisp, young Muscadet or a Gros Plant with this dish.

Serves: 4 people

Preparation time: 10–15 minutes
Cooking time: 20–25 minutes
400g (14oz) celery, cut into thin strips
500g (1lb 2oz) sander, cleaned, filleted and cut into thin slices like smoked salmon
16 sheets filo pastry (readily available in shops) (the recipe makes 8 parcels)
vegetable/sunflower oil for cooking
salt

For the beurre blanc

4 shallots, peeled and chopped
12cl (4fl oz) Muscadet
350g (12oz) unsalted butter, very cold
salt, pepper

Make the *beurre blanc* by sweating the shallots in a frying pan with the wine. Cook on a low heat until the liquid has been reduced to a thick sauce. Add the butter, cut into small cubes, and beat together over a low heat until smooth. Remove from the heat, season with salt and pepper and keep warm on one side.

Preheat the oven to 200°C (400°F, gas mark 6). Heat a little oil in a pan and fry the celery until soft and brown. Take out, drain on kitchen paper and shake a little salt over the strips.

Using the same oil, and adding more if necessary, fry the fish slices very quickly on both sides. When almost completely cooked and just beginning to brown remove from the pan and put to one side.

Lightly oil a sheet of filo pastry and place a second sheet directly on top. Lay a few slices of the fish, topped with a dessertspoonful of the celery, on one half. Oil the edges and fold over the other half of the square. Seal the edges by turning in and pressing lightly to form an envelope. Repeat until 8 parcels have been made. Make 2 small slits in the top of each parcel with a sharp knife.

Place the parcels on a baking tray and cook in the oven for 10–15 minutes until golden brown and crisp.

Serve on a hot plate with the Muscadet *beurre blanc* around the parcels, accompanied by new potatoes and a green vegetable.

few more local specialities, such as the *chocolatier*, Maison Gautier. Here they make *mascarons nantais*, chocolate-covered biscuits which have formed the basis of the chocolate industry in the region since the 17th century. These and *berlingots*, pyramid-shaped fruit- and peppermint-flavoured boiled sweets, first made for Louis XVI, were closely linked to the cocoa and cane sugar imported (as they still are) from the West Indies and the Americas through the port of Nantes.

I also discovered the one local cheese, Curé Nantaise, made on the coast at Cornic from cows' milk. Its tangy flavour, it is generally agreed, goes well with the acidity of Muscadet – just as in Sancerre, further up-river, the goats' milk cheese Crottin de Chavignol goes well with the crisp, herbaceous flavour of the local wines. And there

▲ *Oysters from the Breton coast near Le Croisic: the marriage with the local Gros Plant or Muscadet wines seems pre-ordained.*

► *Artichokes and cabbages in Nantes market; early vegetables, known as* primeurs, *are a speciality of the Loire Valley.*

◄ *One of the great delicacies at the start of a meal in the Loire Valley is fresh, crisp radishes dipped in sea salt.*

was the promise of a local supper dish, *sardines du soir*. Sardines, freshly caught that morning at Saint-Gilles-Croix-de-Vie, are sold to commuters on their way home in the evening.

If the fish market had shown me the rich variety of marine and river life that appears in the Loire's cuisine, the journey to the next region I was to visit – Touraine – revealed the fertility of the soil in the valley. Inland from Nantes the countryside – aptly dubbed the Garden of France – is full of market gardens, many under hectares of glass, which produce *primeurs*, baby vegetables – carrots, leeks, turnips, radishes, cucumbers – for export as well as local consumption.

Further upstream, vineyards cover the high ground back from the river, away from the risk of flooding. In the sparkling wine area of Saumur or the red wine land of Bourgueil hugging the northern bank, the silt-rich plain nourishes different crops: globe artichokes, green beans, celery, peas, asparagus, all vegetables which appear regularly in the local cooking of Anjou and Touraine, either as an accompaniment to fish or meat, or as a *salade tourangelle*, chopped finely and dressed with vinaigrette. On the plateaux and rolling hills away from the river and its Touraine tributaries are vast swathes of cereals, a mass of green then gold in summer, the earth bare brown in winter.

There are other crops from less obvious surroundings. The cliffs along the banks of many of the rivers in Touraine and Anjou are made of tufa, a white calcareous rock which over the centuries has been quarried for building materials, creating a vast honeycomb of caves. Many were used as dwellings, and there are still homes which have a conventional façade but which are built straight into the cliff. Others are used for storing wine or cheese since the constant temperature creates ideal conditions. And still others are used to grow mushrooms.

I visited the Champignonnière du Saut-aux-Loups, a mushroom farm just outside Montsoreau, a short distance from Saumur, one Sunday just before lunch. I had been told that there would be *galipettes* – large Paris mushrooms, filled with herbs and *crème fraîche,* or herbs and meat, or *andouillettes* (a type of pork sausage), then cooked in the wood embers in a large bread oven set into the rock face.

The caves are cool and spacious. Mushrooms, grown in bags of tufa soil, stretch as far as the eye

▼ *The French have long been connoisseurs of mushrooms such as these Pleurotes, but other countries are catching up.*

can see, some small, some enormous, some – called Pleurotes – coloured red and yellow, and others – called Pieds-Bleu – with blue stalks. But the majority are the familiar white Champignons de Paris. There's also a good speciality sideline in Japanese Shii-Take mushrooms, which are said to reinforce the immune system.

The tour ended just in time to see the *galipettes* come out of the oven, smelling of garlic and cheese and herbs. Eaten outside in the sun, with glasses of local red Saumur-Champigny, they made a delicious appetizer, as much for the freshness of those mushrooms as for their fillings.

From here I repaired to lunch in the tiny village of Saint-Germain-sur-Vienne, perched just next to where the Vienne empties into the Loire. Next to the tiny church, with its succession of gargoyles leering over an external arcade, is a proper local restaurant, the Anguille Vagabonde. On a Sunday it is packed with local couples and families, children running and playing, happily ignored by parents and aunts, uncles and grandparents, safe in the knowledge that nobody minds.

I was here to sample the fish that is honoured in the name of the restaurant, *anguille*, eel. Common in all large rivers in France, eels make a regular appearance on riverside dining tables. The Loire version is a rich stew which recalls the *lamproie bordelaise* I had tasted in the kitchens of Château Loudenne (see pages 37 and 44), called here *matelote d'anguille*. *Matelot* means "boatman" and *matelote* refers not to a cut of fish but to the method of cooking. It should, I was told by M Froger, the owner, be cooked in tannic, young red wine (he used the local Chinon), with small onions which darken with the wine, and then topped at the last minute with croûtons. He could have added that huge quantities of garlic, plenty of herbs and slow cooking were equally important requirements. The method, best applied to strong-tasting fish, tenderizes the flesh and allows the red wine to bring out the flavour, not obscure it. The meal is best eaten with the wine used in the cooking, the almost meaty taste of the fish highlighted by the fruitiness of the wine.

Certainly at the Anguille Vagabonde, the Chinon we drank went very happily with the eel, and just as well with the goats' milk cheese that followed. Touraine specializes in pyramid-shaped goats' milk

► *As always in France, sausages form a serious part of the diet for these seasoned gourmets.*

◄ *Loire cheeses, including the flattened pyramid of Valençay and log-shaped, cinder-covered Vazereau.*

cheese. Those from Sainte-Maure are perfect pyramids, while those from Valençay have the top sliced off. The story goes that Napoléon was using a Valençay cheese as a prop for a discussion of tactics over the dinner table, and so keen was he to make a victorious point that he sliced through the top of the cheese with his knife. The shape isn't simply a mark of distinction, it affects the ageing of the cheese: the Sainte-Maure, a complete pyramid, ages more quickly than the chopped-off version preferred in Valençay.

A third style of goats' milk cheese, created by the Guy family in nearby La Roche Clermault and called Vazereau, is shaped like an oblong block, salted and covered with cinders. Vazereau cheeses, matured in the tufa caves near Chinon, come from a part of Touraine that is particularly hallowed in the annals of gourmandise. Just across the valley from La Roche Clermault is La Devinière, birthplace of Rabelais and now a museum and place of pilgrimage. This valley was Rabelais' setting for the battle between Gargantua and the inhabitants of nearby Lerné over *fouaces*, the saffron-flavoured unleavened loaves that were – and still are, thanks to an enterprising baker – a speciality of that village.

Chinon is home to one of the two finest red wines of the Loire (the other is Bourgueil), but the range of styles of Loire Valley wine is truly impressive. Vouvray, a few kilometres east of Tours, produces one of an equally fine pair of sweet white wines (the other comes from the Layon Valley, in Anjou). Touraine is a strong candidate for the title of best region in France for charcuterie, and Vouvray boasts one of the finest charcuterie shops in the country, owned by Jean and André Hardouin. Their produce reaches Fauchon, the Fortnum and Mason of Paris. It crosses the Belgian frontier to arrive in Brussels. It is known the length and breadth of the Loire Valley.

André Hardouin is a dapper, formal man, dressed in a bow tie and the immaculate white jacket of his trade. We talked of his hand-made *andouillette*, which can be grilled or eaten cold, and which, he assured me, goes very well with a sauce made with medium-dry Vouvray (and accompanied with a glass of the same). The same sauce and wine also appear with his *pieds de porc farci*, stuffed pigs' trotters. And there was more Vouvray in the delicious *rillons de veau*, pieces of meat in a Vouvray jelly. We continued with talk of pudding – *boudin* – the white made with ham, pork fillet and cream, the black made with lard, blood and onions. Flour, I was told, in shocked tones at the mere suggestion, is completely forbidden as a binding agent for these puddings.

Despite the strongly local traditions, the theme I heard time and again was that what was so special in Touraine was not its regional dishes. Since this is regarded as almost the home of French cooking, regional dishes here have become national dishes throughout the country. *Coq au vin* and *boeuf bourguignon* both, it is claimed, came originally from here. The special feature is the richness and range of ingredients available. It was with this in mind that I paid my last two visits – one to a chef in a restaurant, one to a cook in her home.

Pierre Koniecka is the young chef at the Auberge de l'Ile at L'Ile Bouchard, east of Chinon on the Vienne. Pierre and his father, who is the *maître d'hôtel*, run a riverside restaurant – one of the rare ones, as they point out to me, in the entire Loire Valley to have a terrace actually overlooking a river. His family is from Picardy, and Pierre has worked in London, so he has come to the Loire cooking as an outsider. To him it is a cuisine of richness with moderation. At the boundary

► *Touraine is rightly seen as one of the very best regions in France for charcuterie, whether made from pork or veal.*

between northern and southern France, the Loire is literally spoilt for choice: "We don't have so much regional dishes here as a choice of all the ingredients of France." He uses the local wine – Chinon – in his cooking, but more importantly he talks about marriages of all the Loire wines with his food: simple matches like *foie gras* and a sweet wine from Quarts de Chaume or Bonnezeaux, or sweet, white Coteaux du Layon wines with a dish of sweetbreads and mushrooms, or an old Chinon red with beef and lamb, or a younger red, Saumur-Champigny perhaps, with richer and heavier fish dishes such as pike.

For Yvette Viemont, at home in Bourgueil,

Cuissot de Lapereau à l'Ancienne

HAUNCH OF RABBIT COOKED IN THE TRADITIONAL WAY

This recipe was given to me by Jean-Claude Rigollet, chef-proprietor of the Au Plaisir Gourmand restaurant in Chinon, one of the most renowned restaurants in the region. It presents a simple way of casseroling rabbit (or hare) which tenderizes the meat and makes a rich winter dish. A mature red Chinon or Bourgueil wine provides a good partner.

Serves: 4 people

Preparation time: 30 minutes
(plus 12 hours marinating time)

Cooking time: 1¼ hours

- 2 rabbit or hare haunches
- 1 rabbit's liver, diced (or ½ a calf's liver)
- 25g (1oz) butter
- 25g (1oz) plain flour
- salt, pepper

For the marinade

- 1 bottle red wine, preferably a Chinon
- 2 shallots, chopped
- 1 carrot, chopped
- 1 large onion, chopped
- 1 sprig thyme
- half bay-leaf, coarsely chopped

Bone the haunches, season with salt and pepper and fill with enough liver to reform the haunch. Tie up each haunch with kitchen string and place next to each other in a casserole dish. Mix together the ingredients for the marinade, pour it over the meat and leave for 12 hours.

The following day, preheat the oven to 180°C (350°F, gas mark 4). Place the casserole dish inside and cook for 1 hour or until the meat is cooked (I like it to be left still slightly pink). Take the meat out of the dish and keep warm to one side.

Simmer the remaining liquid in a pan until it has been reduced by a half and then thicken with the butter and flour. Adjust the seasoning and strain the liquid through a fine sieve.

Place the meat in the casserole dish once again and cover it with the sauce.

In the winter, this would be eaten with local vegetables, but a summer salad would provide a lighter meal in warm weather.

► *Fruit trees at Vertou in the Pays Nantais, part of the "Garden of France".*

there are certainly some local recipes. She cites turnip soup, or the rabbit or wild boar terrines. But, at the same time, she echoes Pierre Koniecka: "There aren't many local dishes because we have everything here – we don't need just to rely on a few ingredients." She does, however, tell me of some dishes that were regularly enjoyed by her generation, and which she still cooks occasionally. One of her favourites is *rouelle de porc*, a dish of pressed pork with shallots in ham jelly, which can be eaten either hot or cold.

Another is, effectively, red wine soup: *bijane*, a dish of croûtons mixed with red wine, water and sugar, and eaten almost as a refreshing drink in hot weather, or during harvest time. And there's the Tourangelle equivalent of *foie gras* – *foie de veau*, a fine terrine of veal cooked slowly with the fat on the outside in a bain-marie – something for special occasions as she puts it.

As for desserts, there are fresh fruit tarts, using local cherries, apples, peaches, pears ("but nobody makes them now, because they can buy them from the *pâtissier*"), and biscuits like the *sables* (see recipes). Or there is fruit in red wine, a standard

dish for any red-wine area. Of course, when I asked Yvette what she would drink with any of these sweets, she gave the same answer: a red Bourgueil.

We don't have to be so restricted, of course, and would probably prefer to drink sweet wines from Vouvray or the Layon Valley. But there is certainly no need to look beyond the Loire for a matching wine, whatever the occasion. And as with wines, so it seems, with the food; there is something there to suit most tastes. No wonder the Loire is the heart of France.

Sables

This is a sweet pastry which can either be made into small biscuits dotted with raisins, or, as Martine Druet, wife of Bourgueil wine producer Pierre-Jacques Druet, makes it, into one large cake decorated with almonds and eaten by breaking pieces off it. Sables can be served with a glass of sparkling Vouvray or with a sweeter wine from Vouvray or Montlouis.

Serves: 6 people

Preparation time: 25 minutes

Cooking time: 5–15 minutes

125g (4½oz) caster sugar

1 tsp salt

1 egg (size 2)

250g (9oz) plain flour

125g (4½oz) unsalted butter

Preheat the oven to 190°C (375°F, gas mark 5). Put the sugar and salt in a mixing bowl. Break the egg into the bowl and beat with a wooden spoon or spatula until the mixture is frothy, light in colour and double the original volume.

Sieve the flour and gradually incorporate it into the mixture with a spoon. Then run the crumbs through your fingers: the texture should be grainy, rather like fine grains of sand – hence the recipe's name.

Turn the mixture out onto a board and fold in the butter, cut into small cubes, piece by piece. Knead well: if the butter has been properly incorporated, the pastry will not stick to your hands.

Form the pastry into a ball and roll it out on a floured surface to a depth of about 1cm.

Cut into biscuit-sized shapes with a pastry cutter, or form into one large cake. Martine Druet puts sliced almonds on her cake and washes the top with egg yolk to enhance the colour and form a crust.

Place the biscuits or cake on a greased baking sheet and cook for 5–10 minutes if biscuits, or 10–15 minutes if one large cake, until pale gold in colour. Take out of the tin and place on a wire cooling tray.

Sables can be served either hot or cold; they are often eaten at the end of the meal with fruit, or mid-morning with coffee or a glass of sparkling wine. The biscuits will keep for 1–2 weeks in an airtight tin.

WINES OF THE LOIRE

As France's longest river, the Loire naturally weaves its way through a landscape of widely varying terrain, soil and climate as it describes a curve north and then west to the sea. Inevitably, the wine produced along its banks and those of its tributaries has an equally protean nature. Here there is none of the homogeneity of Bordeaux or Champagne, but a diversity of styles matched by a versatility of usage – happily there is a Loire Valley wine for every course on the menu, ranging from the driest of white and sparkling wines, to serious reds, frivolous rosés and the luscious, sweet white dessert wines.

Although it may seem strange to bring these wines together as a group, they do have a shared characteristic: a certain lightness, even a freshness, the result of the vineyards' relatively northerly position and the fact that they are influenced as much by the Atlantic Ocean as by the warmer continental climate of eastern France. It is quite likely that, but for the river system of the Loire, wine could not be produced at this latitude. The extra degree or two of warmth lent by the river is enough to push vine-growing from being barely possible to being an undisputed success.

The wines can conveniently be divided into five geographical areas, starting at the river's lofty source in the mountains of central France. Intensive planting is impossible here; the vineyards dotted sparsely over the terrain tend to yield wines which are mainly of local interest. But pockets of charm do exist – the Gamay-based Côtes du Forez is a pleasant example displaying, in a lighter style, all the juicy, fruity character of Beaujolais – but not the high price.

North of Nevers, at the threshold of the lowland Loire Valley, wine production begins in earnest where the vineyards of Sancerre on the west bank face those of Pouilly-sur-Loire on the east. This is the land of Sauvignon Blanc, crisply fresh in Sancerre, fuller and rounder in Pouilly-Fumé; styles that have swept the world and inspired imitators from as far apart as New Zealand

▲ *As well as imposing châteaux, there are innumerable smaller castles, still family-owned, stretching along the Valley.*

and California. These wines admirably partner the region's fish and soft, strong cheeses – the richer Pouilly, with its suggestions of greengages and even tropical fruit, also goes well with white meats: goose, turkey, chicken and capon.

Surprisingly, given the freshness of the wines when young, they can be enhanced by age – those of Pouilly, especially, which transform themselves into wines of some complexity. The same cannot be said for the curiosity of the region: the red and rosé wines made from Pinot Noir, which may be light and fragrant at best, but water-light at worst.

There are patches of viticulture all along the Loire Valley – areas of small production whose wines are rarely seen, such as the rosés and whites of the Coteaux du Giennois and the rosés of Orléans. At a distance from the Loire, the Sauvignons and Pinot Noirs of Ménétou-Salon, Reuilly and Quincy are grown; Ménétou-Salon providing a pleasant alternative to Sancerre, although slightly less crisp.

The third major vine-growing area begins as Touraine and the town of Blois are reached. The wines of Touraine – the reds and rosés based on light, juicy Gamay, the more structured, firmer Cabernets (Franc and Sauvignon), Pinot Noir and Pineau d'Aunis, the whites on crisp, herbaceous Sauvignon Blanc and fresh, creamy Chardonnay, with local curiosities like the Romorantin-based Cheverny (the high acid, very dry Romorantin grape being unique to this region) – are essentially for light, young drinking, with their essential dryness and acidity.

Only in a few, specialized areas is greatness achieved. The white wines of Vouvray are a case in point – dry or sweet (and in lesser years sparkling), they stagger by their acidity when young and by their immensely long life. The only way to drink them is in the year of their birth (when they have the virtue of freshness) or from never less than 10 years old, when even the dry wines develop a honeyed quality, akin to eating quince jelly, or, when sweeter, light treacle. The grape here is the Chenin Blanc, a variety developed and grown extensively in the Loire, capable of producing a remarkable range of wines – both the very dry and the very sweet.

A difficulty encountered with Vouvray – and this is true of wines in so many regions of the Loire – is that much of what is available commercially is of an inferior quality, bottled by large-scale industrial

▼ *Most Loire Valley wines come from tiny vineyard holdings, where grapes are just one of several small crops.*

merchants many miles from the vineyards and made – and sold – at a price.

That this is a fate escaped by Montlouis, Vouvray's neighbour on the opposite bank of the Loire, says more for its relative obscurity than anything else. Montlouis wines are similar in style to Vouvray, generally sweeter rather than drier, and invariably shorter-lived.

The red wines of Bourgueil, Saint-Nicolas-de-Bourgueil and Chinon, in the far west of Touraine, belie the not unreasonable assumption that the Loire, because of its northerly position, can only produce white wines. Here are wines of great stature and complexity. Made from the Cabernet Franc, they can be drunk young, when full of quite tight fruit and tannin, or – much to be preferred – aged over a period of five years or more. With time they develop an enticing character of truffles and vanilla, blackberries and violets. The three

▲ *The rich red wines from Bourgueil bring the flavours of* pot-au-feu du braconnier – *poacher's stew – out of hiding.*

differ in that Bourgueil wines are generally firm with a relatively high tannin content when young, those of Saint-Nicolas are lighter and less able to age, and the wines of Chinon are, appropriately for the home town of Rabelais, more sumptuous and softer, with a feel of taffeta or velvet.

And there's Cabernet Franc to be found to the west, in Anjou, the fourth division of the Loire Valley. Saumur-Champigny is a small area producing reds which are a cross between the youthful freshness of Saint-Nicolas and the softness of Chinon.

Anjou produces other basic reds from Cabernet Franc under the simple Anjou and Anjou-Villages appellations, but in terms of quantity it is the rosés that lead here. A declining market for rosé wines has particularly affected the off-dry Rosé d'Anjou and Cabernet d'Anjou, and only been partly steadied by an interest in the dry Rosé de Loire; the general effect of this trend has been to stimulate local production of red wines.

But Anjou's main claim to fame is its whites, especially its sweet whites. The valley of the tiny Layon tributary, running north into the Loire, has a microclimate similar to the Sauternes region of Bordeaux, with the sunny, misty autumn days needed to encourage the "noble rot" that concentrates the Chenin Blanc grapes and produces superb sweet wines. The whole valley enjoys these late season conditions, but the small vineyards of Bonnezeaux and Quarts de Chaume are particularly favoured. As with any Chenin Blanc-based wine, these need to age for four to five years – when they can taste wonderful with the local pear, peach or apricot tarts.

Curiously, just across from the Layon Valley, on the north bank of the Loire, a small area produces equally fine whites from the Chenin – but these are dry. Savennières and its two sub-appellations of Coulée-de-Serrant and Roche-aux-Moines, have achieved recent justifiable renown: production is small, but prices are still reasonable.

Saumur, as Vouvray, produces sparkling wine from the Chenin Blanc, as well as the Anjou- and Touraine-wide appellation of Crémant de Loire, which may be a combination of Chenin Blanc and Chardonnay – the blend giving greater body and roundness, and making a more attractive wine.

From the provincial capital of Angers, it is no more than an hour's drive to the port of Nantes

▲ *Remarkably for such a diverse landscape, Loire wines do have a shared characteristic: a certain lightness or freshness.*

and not much more to the mouth of the Loire. But that's by the quick route on the north bank; the journey along the south bank takes you through the vineyards of Muscadet, home until recently of one of the world's most popular white wines – a position lost through inferior négociant wines, and inflated prices. Yet, as a name and style, it is still a benchmark for easy-drinking dry whites.

Everywhere you look there are vines, especially in the heartland area between the rivers Sèvre-Nantaise and Maine – this is a stretch of monoculture, rare in the Loire Valley. But while the Melon de Bourgogne, another name for the Muscadet grape, predominates, spare a thought for the lesser Gros Plant du Pays Nantais, which, in its crisp, sometimes tart acidity, for many provides an even more ideal accompaniment to the region's abundant *fruits de mer* than the rather fuller Muscadet.

This last satisfying partnership brings the Loire to the end of its journey. The river's long and sinuous route seems to preclude any attempt to treat the wines made along its length "en masse". They are simply too diverse to be narrowly defined. And yet the Loire and its tributaries are more than a watery link between contrasting landscapes, varieties of cultivation and diverse appellations. It is, for vine-growing here, the indispensable condition, its beneficial, warm microclimate producing delicious wines, linked together by a decided acidity and light, airy, fresh style.

THE LOIRE VALLEY

OTHER SPECIALITIES OF THE REGION AND WINES TO TRY WITH THEM

The Loire Valley is at the heart of French cooking. Here is a region that combines high quality raw materials from the river, ocean and land with classic sauces. Its ideal growing conditions meant that the Loire Valley was the first to cultivate products now taken for granted in French cuisine, including lettuces, peas, artichokes, plums, pears and melons. And with its endless list of river fish – carp, trout, tench, pike, shad, salmon – it is hardly surprising that **beurre blanc**, the greatest of sauces for fish, was created near Nantes.

▲ *Fish in the Talensac market at Nantes, a scene of organized chaos every morning lasting for just one hour so that the fish are sold when freshest.*

In Anjou, shad, carp and tench are filled with sorrel – **à l'oseille** – or stuffed and then cooked in a dry white wine, such as a Savennières, for **farçie à l'angevine**. In Touraine, eels in red wine are accompanied by prunes. There are *matelotes* (fish stews) using local red or white wine, and fish dipped in batter and then deep fried: **friture de la Loire**.

To drink: *wines familiarly partnered with fish are the dry whites of Sancerre and Pouilly-Fumé, Touraine's Sauvignon Blanc and Anjou's Savennières and Muscadet, but locals often drink young, tannic, red wines with these dishes, especially with richer fish such as eel.*

Delightful, old-fashioned restaurants and bars in the centre of Nantes serve good selections of **fruits de mer** – lobsters, prawns, shrimps, oysters and crabs – as well as sea bass, red mullet, sole and sardine dishes, with *beurre blanc* as the standard accompaniment.

To drink: *the local Muscadet and Gros Plant, with their almost tart acidity and crisp, light, fresh flavours are ideal.*

Anjou and Touraine in particular specialize in charcuterie. From Touraine come **rillons** (savoury pork nuggets), **rillettes** (a terrine of pork, carrots and shallots marinated in Vouvray or Montlouis) and **andouillettes** (sausages made with chitterlings). **Terrine de lapin aux pruneaux** is a speciality of Amboise, again using prunes from Tours; the rabbit meat is mixed with Vouvray and bound together with egg.

To drink: *red wine is the best choice, perhaps an Anjou-Villages or a wine from Saumur-Champigny, Chinon or Bourgueil, one that is comparatively young and therefore tannic. Alternatively, try the local sweet and medium-sweet white wines of Vouvray and Montlouis.*

Meat and game dishes abound in the Loire Valley, especially in the mountains at the source of the river. In recognition of local practices, Orléanais has **pot-au-feu du braconnier** – poacher's stew – for which the rabbit is slowly casseroled with root vegetables and bacon. Partridge, hare and venison are braised or roasted and then served with garden vegetables.

In the river valley and to the north near Chartres, *pâtés* are traditionally made from the hare, thrush and lark. The corn-fed chickens of Loches in Touraine are braised with milk, cream and onions for **geline lochoise**, while ducklings, the speciality of Nantes, become **canard au Muscadet** – roast duck with a sauce of Muscadet, shallots and cream.

To drink: any of the red Loire wines are suitable – particularly those from Chinon and Bourgueil. If possible, choose one that is rich and mature, although younger, tannic wines go well with pâtés.

From the Massif Central come lamb dishes such as **gigot brayaude** – leg of lamb studded with garlic and braised in white wine with vegetables and herbs, while from near the mouth of the river comes **fressure vendéen** (also called **lard nantais**). For this dish, the pig's liver, heart, lungs and spleen are cooked in red wine and served cold. Haunch of veal is cooked with Saumur white wine for **cul de veau à l'angevine**; sparkling Saumur with veal kidneys becomes **rognons de veau saumuroise**.

To drink: a red wine, either the rich, smooth wines of Chinon and Bourgueil, the lighter Pinot Noir reds of Sancerre, or the young, fruity wines of the Côtes du Forez in the upper Loire.

Soupe tourangelle is a summer vegetable soup made with **primeurs** – the first vegetables of the season – plus root vegetables, bacon, chicken stock and bread.

The Loire Valley's cheeses can be neatly divided into those from the mountains of the upper river, and those from the pasture land along the lower reaches. The Massif Central is the source of famous cows' milk varieties such as the **Fourme de Montbrison**, a firm, slightly bitter cheese from Forez. In the lower Loire Valley, both cows' and goats' milk cheeses are plentiful. **Caillebotte** is a mild cheese, while **Bondaroy au Foin** from Pithiviers in the Orléanais, wrapped in straw for curing, is more tangy. **Olivet Bleu** and **Vendôme Bleu** come from north of the Loire, **Crémet Nantais**, soft and creamy, hails from the Pays Nantais. Perhaps the most famous of the Loire's goats' milk cheeses is **Crottin de Chavignol** from Sancerre, but there is also **Chabichou**, truncated and cone-shaped, with a blue rind. **Gien** from south of Orléans is firm and ash-coated.

To drink: with milder cheeses, try a red wine such as a Chinon or a Sancerre, soft and mature. For stronger varieties, white wines can be better, such as Pouilly-Fumé and Sancerre, with crisp acidity to counter the tanginess of the cheese. And for blue cheese: try a sweet wine from Vouvray or Montlouis, or from the Coteaux du Layon in Anjou.

Anjou and Touraine are regions filled with mouth-watering pastries, while the Pays Nantais specializes in filled crêpes. From the upper Loire come **Sanciau** or **Crapiau**, thick pancakes, either sweet or savoury. **Gâteau Pithiviers** is puff-pastry filled with frangipane, while **La tart aux abricots à la crème de Pithiviers** combines ground almonds and rum. **Pain d'épices de Pithiviers** joins cinnamon, honey and crystallized fruit in cake form. **Tarte tatin**, France's celebrated upside-down caramelized fruit tart comes from the Solonge, south of Orléans; the tart is named after the Tatin sisters who created it in the 19th century.

In Touraine, many of the tarts and pastries are fruit-based, but there is also **pêches de Touraine à la royale au Vouvray pétillant** – peaches and strawberries with sparkling Vouvray. **Chicolle** is the Tourangelle version of peaches in red wine. Anjou is the home of Cointreau and therefore of **soufflé glacé au Cointreau**, which comes served with aniseed biscuits. **Crémets**, made with whipped cream and stiff egg whites are produced in heart-shaped moulds and served with strawberries.

To drink: for many, the sweet wines of the Layon Valley - especially the luscious Bonnezeaux and Quarts de Chaume would be ideal with fruity puddings and pancakes, but the dry sparkling wines of Saumur and Vouvray are also served as a counterpoint to sweet food, especially pastries.

▼ *A reminder that the Pays Nantais, as part of Brittany, is in cider country.*

LANGUEDOC

A N D

ROUSSILLON

The entrance to Monsieur Poudou's house is easily missed. A cross between a ramshackle garden shed and a garage stands hemmed in on one side by the road, on the other by a thick line of trees. Only the small sign saying "*miel*" – honey – and the name of the place, Boysède, catch the eye.

I stopped the car and listened to the sound of running water, a frenzy of birdsong and the clatter of a gate being opened somewhere along the side of the building. Through it emerged a small man, over 70, but whose eyes shone with passion and enthusiasm, who rushed me down a narrow path, through a shed full of ancient tools, parts of motor cars and equipment for bee-keeping, into the most dusty, comfortable little study.

Every surface was covered with paraphernalia, every wall lined with those brown-covered French paperbacks that simply dare you to open them. Above M Poudou's desk hung a faded oil painting – a Claude landscape crossed with a Landseer. The desk itself, layered with papers that might have been left untouched for years, was, it appeared, laid out so that whatever M Poudou wanted was just at hand to illustrate his subject – honey.

Honey may seem a far cry from wine, but in the Corbières, in southern Languedoc, the two are never far apart. The Aude département is home to over 2,000 bee-keepers and there are as many signs for honey as there are for wine in this isolated mountain region. Where there are no vines there are the flowers of the *garrigue* – the semi-scrubland that covers the hills – and herbs, the source of the finest honey of all.

Honey, M Poudou told me, has its roots in the oldest civilizations of the Corbières. The Romans made hydromel, mead – which is still made locally today – sometimes adding it to their grape wine as a sweetener; and in the valley around Narbonne, the ancient capital of the region, they made honey itself. Today *miel de Narbonne* is one of the most prized styles in France.

We sampled, using tiny plastic dippers to take small, incredible, heart-stopping portions of the most wonderful honey I have ever tasted. Top of

► M Poudou, dedicated beekeeper, is one of over 2,000 honey producers in the Aude département.

▲ Preparing the smoke from dried mountain herbs; even when being smoked out of their hives, the bees are subdued pleasantly with delicious smells.

◄ M Poudou inspects the hives. His bees travel throughout the mountains feeding on pollen from the herbs and flowers of the garrigue, *and reaching as far as the coastal* maquis.

the quality league are two that represent the smell of the Corbières more than any other: one from rosemary – *miel de romarin* – very aromatic and perfumed, rich and almost overpowering, the other from thyme – *miel de thym* – smoother, subtler, a lighter honey altogether.

Both these styles are derived from the *garrigue*, where the gorse bushes flower in a blaze of yellow at the height of the honey season in May and June. There is also lavender honey from the *garrigue*, very smooth but perhaps just a little too sweet for my taste, and, from the flowers amongst the sparse pine vegetation of the coastal *maquis,* comes a variety that M Poudou was keen to convince me had a salt tang.

Outside once again, we looked across the valley, dripping from a recent shower. The River Alsou rushes past and, indeed, through the house, which is still a mill, powering an ancient electricity generator. The Moulin de Boysède dates back in parts to the 8th century, the original mill, M Poudou assured me, having been constructed by order of the Emperor Charlemagne.

Just before I left, we scrambled up the steep hillside just across the road from the mill to pick large stalks of rosemary, thyme and lavender growing among a small patch of vines, beside a fig tree. "Take them with you", he said, "and smell them as you taste the honey." He paused for his parting words – a short recitation: "We grow figs to protect the house, pomegranates to give the inhabitants fertility, olives to give them food, and vines to give them joy." Then it was time to move on.

The valley of the River Alsou is narrow, tall cliffs close in until, just upstream from Boysède, they create one of the gorges for which the Corbières is famous: sheer skyscrapers of rock, a few trees hanging, improbably, halfway up, a tiny field or patch of vegetation clinging at the bottom to the riverbank. And just downstream is Lagrasse, capital of the Val d'Orbieu region – describing itself, not inaccurately, as one of the most beautiful villages of France – dominated by the abbey of Sainte-Marie d'Orbieu, founded in the 8th century and still a thriving community.

Lagrasse is one of the centres of the Corbières wine region. From the road which descends into the village the red pantiled roofs glow warmly in the sun, the tower of the abbey church dominates

Pain d'Epices au Miel

SPICY HONEY BREAD

Spicy honey bread is found widely in the Corbières – this recipe comes from Mme Poudou, using the honey from her husband's bees. It is delicious by itself or spread with a little butter or honey and, depending on the time of day, can be eaten either with a cup of tea or with a sweet Muscat wine from the Languedoc – or even with a mug of hydromel (mead), if the opportunity arises.

Serves: 6 people

Preparation time: 15 minutes (plus 24 hours resting time)

Cooking time: 1½ hours

1kg (2lb 4oz) plain flour

2 heaped tsp bicarbonate of soda

2 level tsp nutmeg

2 level tsp allspice

2 level tsp ginger

1 level tsp salt

pinch of black pepper

1kg (2lb 4oz) very soft, melted or runny honey

60cl (1pt) milk, approximately

2 tbsp olive oil

Put all the dry ingredients in a mixing bowl and stir together well. Make a hollow in the centre and pour in the honey. Incorporate the honey slowly, adding the milk gradually at the same time, until the mixture forms a thick, smooth paste.

Mix in the olive oil thoroughly and then leave the pastry to rest for 24 hours in the fridge.

The following day, preheat the oven to 180°C (350°F, gas mark 4). Spread the pastry evenly in a 20cm (8in) rectangular cake tin, place in the oven and cook for 1½ hours, until well-risen and firm to the touch.

Remove the cake from the tin and leave to cool on a wire cooling tray.

◄ *The town of Lagrasse, dominated by its abbey church, clusters next to the River Alsou.*

from one side, while two ancient bridges span the river. Despite its billing, Lagrasse has not been spoilt by tourism. On the wide boulevard that skirts the main centre a café is the only sign of life. Here, from early morning onwards, locals order glasses of Rouge, the rough red wine that in more skilled hands becomes Corbières, while – to a man and woman – they smoke.

In the tortuous village streets, a few small shops – the butcher, the baker, a newspaper shop – serve the small community. Turning a corner leads, as often as not, to the large parish church with its Romanesque windows; flowers are everywhere – overflowing from window boxes or hanging baskets, in pots on either side of a doorway. And from behind every gate comes a sequence of fierce barks as you pass up each alleyway.

Vines are almost the only crop that the poor, stony soil on the hills surrounding the village can yield. While the coastal plain towards the Mediterranean is profuse with fruit trees – with cherries, melons, apricots, peaches, pears, figs and medlars – here in the remote mountains, the only crops apart from grapes are to be found in the small vegetable gardens attached to every house, and on the occasional fruit tree growing in someone's front garden. Only when the valley broadens out towards Lézignan and Narbonne do richly fertile fields appear. Here, too, are found olive trees.

This contrast between relative poverty and richness in natural resources divides not only the steep, clefted mountains of the Languedoc from its coastal plains, but also, to some extent, separates Languedoc from the neighbouring province of Roussillon, which stretches from north of Perpignan down to the Spanish border.

At France's southernmost tip, Roussillon benefits

► *The Minervois vineyards spread out in the flat valley of the River Aude, and rise into the hills in the distance.*

▲ *Appropriately, olive trees surround L'Olivbo, the olive oil cooperative at Bize.*

from even longer, hotter periods of sunshine, producing orchards burdened with fruit, fields crammed with vegetables, and leaving every table laden with a vibrant cuisine which has in many ways adopted the bright colours – peppers, tomatoes – and spicy flavourings of Catalonia. And, to the

south, are the dense game-rich forests of the Pyrennees – a far cry indeed from the stony, barren beauty of the Corbières Mountains.

While those living in Roussillon can dine on *bouillinada* (a Catalan *bouillabaisse*) or grilled mussels, away from the coast in Languedoc, salt cod may be the only fish available. In the Ardèche, in northern Languedoc, quantities of *marrons glacés* are now made, but, in earlier, more spartan times, when much was made of the little available, these chestnuts were a staple food and not a luxury for the sweet-toothed.

The coasts of Roussillon and the Languedoc, in particular, may show an eclectic mix of flavourings from Latin and even Arabic cuisine, but the typical southern French seasonings still predominate – the garlic, herbs and olive oil. The cooperative of L'Olivbo at Bize, in the wine region of Minervois, is the only one in the area. A small concern, handling just 125 tonnes of olives a year, it still represents big business in a region where most farmers have only a few olive trees and press their crop for their own consumption.

M Buira, the director, took me round. A young man, talking fast, and as passionate about olives as M Poudou is about honey, he showed me a map of the Mediterranean with the areas of olive production marked in an appropriate yellowy-green: Spain, all of Italy from Tuscany southwards, parts of Greece, the Levant and North Africa. In France there are two areas – the coastal strip of Provence, and this small semi-circular area in the Aude. Outside this small region the mountains make the climate too cool: this is the frontier between the blessed lands of the olive and those beyond.

The time-consuming manual work required (three crops of olives are harvested each year) explains why so few farmers are willing to work olive groves. The first harvest in September is for the green olives, the second, in November, for black – both are eaten whole, as condiments or ingredients in the local cuisine. The harvest of olives for oil takes place in December, by which time the fruit is extremely ripe and this, believes M Buira, is what sets the French olive oils apart – even from the great Italian olive oils of Tuscany, where the higher altitudes and cooler autumns mean the fruit never achieves quite the same amount of ripeness. Expect a French olive oil, whether from the Aude, from the neighbouring region of Hérault, or from Provence, to be fuller and have less acidity than one from Italy; and the lower the acidity of the oil, the finer it will be. Also expect to find a profusion of different qualities – from the basic Fine, through Extra, Extra Fine, and Vierge (virgin) to Vierge Extra.

M Buira adopts a religious tone as he talks about the place of the olive in Mediterranean culture, citing the belief that it was the first tree to appear on earth, and recalling that the olive branch was the first sign that the waters of the Flood were receding. It is the symbol of peace – it is, he concludes triumphantly, more than a food, it is a culture. To add to this, I am reminded that olive oil is low in cholesterol, and therefore reduces the risk any Frenchman courts of liver problems; and I am assured with great conviction that olive oil also helps the nervous system, and keeps the digestion

► *Goats' cheese preserved in a golden suspension of olive oil is sold at L'Olivbo cooperative.*

▼ *Mme Donnet – guardian of traditional cheese-making in the Hautes Corbières – with her Brebis.*

generally in good working order.

That night, I tried a simple salad full of local ingredients: black olives, tomatoes, chopped onions, anchovies and green salad leaves, topped with a dressing of olive oil, not as part of a vinaigrette but, as is the local custom, with lemon juice. This combination has a lightness and delicacy that vinaigrette never has, and allows the softness and smoothness of the oil to come through and keep my liver in trim.

Naturally, I was drinking Corbières, but I had begun with another local wine, one which outside the Midi – the French term for the south of France, west of Provence – is usually drunk with dessert or on its own at the end of a meal, but which here, like Sauternes in Bordeaux, is treated as an apéritif. Sweet Muscats are produced in many different regions in the Midi and the Rhône Valley. The most familiar is the Rhône Valley's Muscat de Beaumes-de-Venise but, locally, there is the more attractive – because less blowsy and over-perfumed – Muscat de Saint-Jean-de-Minervois which, with nuts and olives, makes a relaxing way to start a meal.

And to round it off? The only way to remain in tune with the Languedoc is to eat either goats' or sheep's milk cheese – a finishing touch preferred to sweet desserts. Neighbouring Roussillon favours fruit at the end of a meal, especially compotes from locally grown apricots, peaches or cherries.

The pasture land of much of the Languedoc is not rich enough for cows to graze, but in the high lands of the Hautes Corbières there are mountain pastures above the line of the vine and the olive where the hardier goat and sheep can range, and here a few producers are at work making small quantities of goats' milk cheese, as well as one making a sheep's milk variety.

The next day I made my ascent to these stony pastures, up the beautiful valley of the Dagne, due west of Lagrasse and further into the mountains. Every village has its castle – recalling the earlier, troubled times of a region now peaceful and remote, with vines on the valley floor and rough grassland and scrub on the rocky slopes.

At the end of a track that leads from the hamlet of Villetritouls, halfway up the hillside, is the farm of the Donnets. The family comes from the Cévennes, in northern Languedoc, where making goats' cheese is a great local tradition, but, in the Corbières, they are the guardians of another valuable custom, as possibly the only producers of sheep's milk cheese – known locally as Brebis. Their neighbours, also sheep-farmers, continue to sell their animals for meat, but the Donnets' revival of traditional methods – they use only unpasteurized milk, for instance – has taken their cheese as far as Paris. In a firm division of labour, M Donnet looks after the animals, collecting the milk each day – as little as one litre per ewe – which Mme Donnet then turns into cheese and a variety of related products: cream, yoghurt and *crème fraîche*

▼ *Goats at Carrus, feeding on the stony mountain pastures of the Corbières.*

(thickened cream, with a noticeably sharp flavour; the sheep's milk variety is much richer than that from cows' milk).

We descended, glasses of sweet, red Grenache in hand, down narrow wooden steps into the cellar where the cheeses mature at a cool 12°C. The taste of milk in the very young cheese develops in a matter of weeks into a deliciously soft-flavoured cheese, much less bitter than any goats' milk variety; and one equally happy, I discovered, to partner both the Grenache (like a younger version of the great *vin doux naturel* of Banyuls, further south in Roussillon) and a much drier red Corbières. The sweet wine has an official place in Mme Donnet's fromagerie – she washes her small, round Tomette des Corbières cheeses with it, which gives them a faint orange glow.

But not far away, to the south of Lagrasse at Carrus, it is goats' milk cheese that preoccupies Jeannette and Bernard Gaschard. For them, it is more than a business – it has become a crusade. Getting to their house is itself an exercise in faith, which would have been sorely tried had it not been for the exhortations painted on the narrow track. "Only five minutes to Carrus" was the one I needed as I topped yet another mountain ridge and looked down into a typical *garrigue* landscape, knee-deep in a yellow haze of gorse, with stony, sun-drenched hills stretching into the distance. Far below, I could just make out a large barn and what seemed to be a ruin, but not another sign of life appeared.

At first sight, there seemed to be no way down, then the track took a nosedive, straight through a grove of oak trees, past the barn and up to the ruin – which turned out to be the Gaschards' home, half of it still under reconstruction, but the other half with the ample proportions and solid comfort of a substantial farmhouse.

Here was tranquillity indeed, as we sat on the bench outside the house taking bites of goats'

cheese and drinking from a demijohn of red wine.

They sell cheese at all stages of development – from Fromage Frais onwards. This Fromage Frais, deliciously light, with a bubbly grainy texture (because the cheese is matured in linen) was made even more exceptional when I was persuaded to add a little *miel de romarin* – rosemary honey.

Then we moved on to shaped cheeses, starting with a three-day old cheese, light and fresh with the taste of milk still lingering, followed by a 15-day old one, still soft and with not too much of that bitter taste that does seem to creep into some older goats' milk cheeses. Both these cheeses went well with the red wine, rough and full-bodied, being poured from the apparently bottomless demijohn. But once we reached a much older cheese, matured for several weeks, dry and with hints of blue veining through it, the tannin in the red could not cope. This was the moment for white Corbières, a rarer style of wine, but, with its full

◀ *The fundamentals of life, shown on a fresco in the Corbières.*

Tarte Salée au Fromage de Chèvre Frais

TART WITH GOATS' MILK CHEESE

This recipe was created by Jeannette Gaschard, who produces goats' milk cheeses at Carrus, high in the mountain pastures of the Corbières. A simple dish, giving you the bright, clear tastes of the south, it goes well with the young, red wines of the Languedoc – a Coteaux du Languedoc or a Fitou. The recipe for pâte brisée *(shortcrust pastry) can be found in the chapter on Alsace, on page 21.*

Serves: 6 people

Preparation time: 20 minutes

(plus 15 minutes to make the *pâte brisée*)

Cooking time: 1 hour 10 minutes

250g (9oz) *pâte brisée*

4 eggs (size 2)

200g (7oz) young, fresh goats' milk cheese

garnish to taste (Mme Gaschard suggests sliced tomatoes and mushrooms, olives, anchovies and onion rings)

salt, pepper

Preheat the oven to 200°C (400°F, gas mark 6). Roll out the *pâte brisée* into a circle about 3mm (⅛in) thick and line a 30cm (12in) flan case. Cover the flan case with greaseproof paper held down with a few china baking balls, place in the oven and bake blind for 15 minutes. This will prevent the flan base from becoming soggy.

Remove the flan case from the oven and leave on one side to cool. Adjust the oven temperature to 220°C (425°F, gas mark 7).

Beat the eggs together and season with salt and pepper. Stir in the goats' milk cheese and spread the mixture over the base of the flan case. Place in the oven and cook for 15 minutes.

Remove the flan case from the oven and turn the temperature down to 180°C (350°F, gas mark 4). Cover the flan evenly with the various garnishes, return it to the oven and cook for 40 minutes, until the top is light brown.

taste and only light acidity, a much happier partner.

After this extensive cheese tasting I fully intended to forget lunch altogether. But, on leaving the little village of Rieux-en-Val, below the high pastures of the Gaschards' house, I found myself tempted to stop by a crowd of cars and the cooking smells coming from a dilapidated farmhouse by the side of the road. "La Horte", it announced itself, "Restaurant à la Ferme". I went in, and was offered a menu that, for 120 francs, promised me four courses plus wine – the sort of menu that visitors often believe can be found anywhere in France, but is in fact quite rare. By wine, I discovered, it meant two whole bottles even more local than a Corbières, bearing the designation Vin de Pays du Val de Dagne – one red, one white, which, while hardly sophisticated, were ideally suited to the local food on offer.

However, the first course, *salade tiède*, warm salad with a blue cheese sauce, brought me back to the sweet Grenache that I had sipped earlier, on the principle that sweet wines go well with blue cheese. Then there was salmon with a saffron, *crème fraîche* and red pimento sauce – again a reminder that the Midi is not far from Catalonia – which suited the white wine's somewhat heavy and oily character. *Magrets de canard* (duck's breast, traditionally from a bird fattened for *foie gras*) was next – a dish illustrating the cross-fertilization between the cuisine of Bordeaux and the south-west, dominated by duck and goose, and that of Languedoc. With this I drank the red wine from the restaurant's own vineyard: soft, quite light, with a pleasant, herby taste. The Donnets' sheep provided the last course: a light *crème fraîche* of sheep's milk, served with local strawberries.

The only way to follow a lunch like that is – no, not to sleep – but to visit a canning factory. Not that M Esquines' *conserverie* at Douzens is any ordinary canning factory – not when he is putting *foie gras*, hams, turkey liver *pâté* and, above all, the region's speciality, *cassoulet*, into tins, using recipes that, as the cups and certificates above his desk testify, are constantly winning awards.

If any region can lay claim to being the home of the thick haricot bean stew called *cassoulet*, said M Esquines, it is the Aude département. The name of the dish is supposed to derive from the *cassol*

▼ *Fruit and vegetables on display in Lagrasse. The selection may be small, but the quality – and taste – are marvellous.*

▲ *Tinned products from M Esquines. His* cassoulet au confit de canard *has been voted the best in France.*

d'Issel, a clay cooking pot made in the village of Issel near the village of Castelnaudary. And *cassoulet de Castelnaudary* is, for any who live in the Aude, the authentic original of a dish whose ownership is now claimed by Toulouse, Gascony, Périgord – and, it seems, almost any point in the southwest of France. For the Audois, goose and duck are the only meats allowed to grace the pot, as well as sausage – charcuterie plays a prominent role in Languedoc, particularly the large pork sausages from Toulouse – while simple pork and ham are only fit for poor imitations of this venerable dish.

Cassoulet is true farmhouse cooking, hearty fare typical of the Languedoc whose dishes, economical and generally uncomplicated, reflect the harsher existence of earlier years. Three vital elements ensure a superlative taste. The first is the choice of beans (the haricot bean – known in Languedoc as *le lingot* – is considered to be the most authentic sort); the second essential is patience and the third slow cooking. The pot is left uncovered so that a skin forms, which is then broken and stirred back into the pot (traditionally the cook uses the magic number of seven, breaking and stirring seven times).

The general advice is to start the day beforehand by soaking the beans (see recipes) – and an equally firm belief is that any *cassoulet* lunch (which involves consumption in considerable quantities) must be taken on a day when nothing else whatever is to be done.

This was certainly the view held by M Esquines, whose *cassoulet au confit de canard* had just won a national competition run by Gault et Millau – a magazine rivalling the Michelin guides. And while he makes a lesser *cassoulet le vendangeur* – harvester's *cassoulet* – using pork, it is the *cassoulet* using duck

Cassoulet de Castelnaudary

BEAN STEW FROM CASTELNAUDARY

This version of the classic dish of the Midi was described by the French novelist Anatole France as the "God the Father" of all cassoulets*. A hearty winter dish, it should be accompanied by copious quantities of red wine – a Corbières or a Minervois – and followed by plenty of time for relaxation.*

Serves: 8 people

Preparation time: 20 minutes (plus 12 hours soaking time)

Cooking time: 7 hours, approximately

- 2kg (4lb 7oz) dried haricot beans
- 1 bouquet garni of thyme and parsley
- 1 large onion, chopped roughly
- 2 cloves
- 2 large carrots, cut lengthwise
- 2 large leeks (preferably white), chopped into 1in lengths
- 1 duck or goose (goose produces a fattier dish)
- 2 cloves garlic, peeled
- 400g (14oz) streaky bacon
- 1 large pork sausage, flavoured with herbs or garlic
- 4 tomatoes, chopped roughly and de-seeded
- 120cl (2pt) meat stock, approximately (beef stock is best, because not too fatty)
- 100g (4oz) lard
- 100g (4oz) breadcrumbs
- salt

Soak the beans in cold water overnight. The following day, drain the beans, rinse in cold water and place in a large saucepan or casserole dish. Add the bouquet garni, the onion, cloves, carrots and leeks. Cover with cold water. Cook over a medium heat, keeping just on the boil, for 1½ hours or until almost cooked.

In the meantime, preheat the oven to 190°C (375°F, gas mark 5), season the duck or goose with salt, place in a greased roasting tin and cook in the oven for 1 hour, turning once, so that the meat is partly roasted.

Adjust the oven temperature to 170°C (325°F, gas mark 3). Rub the inside of a large earthenware pot with the cloves of garlic and line the pot with the bacon. Joint the goose or duck and place in the bottom of the pot. Prick the sausage and place it next to the joints of meat. Add the vegetables and pour over enough stock to cover the ingredients. Season to taste (the dish may already be salty enough) and then dot the top ingredients with the lard, chopped into lumps.

Place the pot, uncovered, in the oven and cook gently for 4½ hours, breaking and stirring in the skin that forms on top at least 7 times. Sprinkle the breadcrumbs over the top and cook for a further 50 minutes, without stirring, until the breadcrumbs are golden, but not burnt.

Serve straight from the pot, followed by a light salad. The *cassoulet* can easily be reheated for subsequent meals.

▲ *Repair work requires a keen eye and infinite patience, but the ample catch makes the labour worthwhile.*

▲ *Houses and fishing nets vie for the waterfront at the village of Bages.*

of which he is most proud. That and another local dish which he also puts into his distinctive black- and gold-labelled tins: *frejinat*. This is the local name for fricassée of pork, a stew which traditionally employed most parts of the animal, cooked in wine and with a tomato sauce flavoured with peppers and vinegar; colours and tastes reminiscent of Spanish cooking. Here, top quality ingredients are used, but the dish has its origins in an older, peasant cuisine, where poor cuts of possibly tough meat were marinated in wine to give a boost of flavour and greater tenderness.

With all these thoughts of meat dishes, it is easy to forget that the Corbières also has a Mediterranean coastline, the region's vast stretches of vines growing right up to the water's edge in the area of Sigean. The Etangs, huge, almost completely enclosed seawater basins, are a feature of this length of coastline, a continuation of the marsh landscape of the Camargue, on Languedoc's eastern border. The Etang de Sigean (also called the Etang de Bages, depending on which of the two towns you come from) has reed-fringed beaches, with, in the west, a backdrop of the Corbières Mountains and, in the east, the hill of La Clape, home to some of the best Coteaux du Languedoc wines.

It was in the small resort town of Bages, on the shore of the lake, that I met a chef with an obsession – and a restaurant devoted to it. Didier Marty is owner of Le Portanel restaurant, which hangs off the cliff-side overlooking the little harbour of Bages – a scene that brings to mind the villages of southern Cornwall. M Marty is a fisherman, and a chef of 28 years standing. From the Etang in front of his restaurant he nets *anguilles* – eels. His enthusiasm is so great that he has devised a whole menu, bar the dessert, devoted to this local delicacy, with suggestions for wines.

So, you can start with a terrine of eel, home-smoked eel, or eels marinated in sage. With this he recommends a dry Muscat of a style made in the Val d'Orbieu in Corbières: alcoholic, but with a taste of spice and honey. Then there are sautéed eels served with a parsley sauce and accompanied either by a white from the Corbières, fresh and fragrant in the modern style, or by a full-bodied, slightly tannic rosé from neighbouring Minervois.

Continuing the surfeit, we pass on to eels in a piquant sauce, a richer dish which is well partnered by a full-bodied red wine from La Clape. Then it's on to a *bourride* of eel (a dish for which the fish is cooked in wine and served with a sauce thickened with egg yolk – a recipe originating in Sète, a port town near Montpellier). Again, this is best served

▲ *Didier Marty, eel expert and owner of Le Portanel restaurant.*

with a red wine, possibly a fruity Corbières. As a *coup de grâce* – and as you head for exhaustion – there is civet of eel, a sautée of eel with shallots, onions and tomatoes, topped by a red wine sauce, and washed down by an oak-aged Corbières. Finally, before sliding under the table, you are offered light honey mousse with a thyme sauce.

Didier Marty is an outgoing character, full of *bonhomie*, but he became a little reticent when I enquired how many people actually went right through this menu, assuring me it was "very light", rather than offering numbers. But if you want a menu with a theme, here it most definitely is.

There are other fish, of course, on the menu at Le Portanel, as befits a Mediterranean region: turbot, sole, calamary, all of which arrive at Port-la-Nouvelle a few miles further south. There are oysters from the Etang de Leucate, which is bordered by the Fitou wine-growing region just to the south, and smoked fish – salmon, trout, red mullet and tuna – which he serves with dry Muscat.

Watching the setting sun cast its reflections over the waters of the Etang, I wondered at the extreme contrasts which Languedoc and Roussillon present – the one offering fairly simple fare, the other a piquant cuisine, bursting with colour, heady with southern influences – and at the division within Languedoc itself: this piece of Mediterranean coast devoted entirely to fish, the mountains a few miles inland hardly feeling the influence of the sea; and how, in a very satisfactory way, the local wines manage to bridge these gaps.

Brandade Nîmoise

BRANDADE FROM NIMES

"Brandade" *is the term for salt cod prepared by pounding or softening the flesh with olive oil, milk and (as an optional extra) garlic, to give a creamy-textured mixture. This recipe, from Nîmes, seems to suggest that fish from the Atlantic were traditionally traded in the Languedoc for other goods, since cod is not part of the Mediterranean catch. Try a white wine with this dish: a soft, low acid Clairette de Bellegarde, a Picpoul de Pinet, or a light, unoaked Corbières or Minervois.*

Serves: 8-12 people

Preparation time: 20 minutes (plus 24 hours soaking time)

Cooking time: 30 minutes

500g (1lb 2oz) salt cod

20cl (7fl oz) milk

1 clove garlic

20cl (7fl oz) olive oil

salt, pepper

Soak the cod for 24 hours in cold water (halve the time if the fish has already been filleted). For the soaking to be most effective, either change the water regularly (about every hour) or leave the fish under running water for at least the first 3–4 hours.

Boil the milk and then put aside to cool. Flake the fish into a thick-bottomed copper pan or a lined cast-iron pan and place over a low heat.

Add the garlic, finely chopped, and then begin to pour in the olive oil, a few drops at a time, while mashing the mixture with a spatula.

When about half the oil has been incorporated, add half the cooled milk, again just a few drops at a time. Continue to stir in the oil and milk, little by little, until the mixture can absorb no more liquid and is a firm-textured paste. Season with salt and pepper to taste.

Serve simply, with plain boiled potatoes.

WINES OF LANGUEDOC AND ROUSSILLON

As a wine region, the Midi is vast, stretching from Nîmes in the east to Carcassonne in the west, reaching up to touch the Massif Central in the north and down to meet the Pyrenees in the south. The vines follow the curve of the Mediterranean coastline in a great arc as it sweeps south from the Rhône delta to the Spanish border; they ascend from the placid coastal plain around Nîmes and Montpellier to dramatic mountains which approach closer and closer to the sea the further south you travel. Over half of the land in Languedoc and Roussillon which can be cultivated is covered with vines, making it the largest wine-growing region in the world – and it is a prolific producer.

The Midi is certainly the land of the European "wine lake" – and a ready contributor to the more recently formed lake of surplus distilled wine. This trend of overproduction, in effect, of putting quantity before quality, began over a century ago when vines were replanted following the phylloxera epidemic, which devastated existing vineyards. Since then, most producers have expended all their energy on producing the most basic *vin* very *ordinaire*. Yet, in the last few decades, as the national market for large quantities of inferior quality wine has died, ancient wine-growing areas have re-emerged to assert themselves as producers of excellent, good value wines – given the right investment of skills, money and equipment.

As a result, the Midi is now the source of some of France's most enjoyable wines – enjoyable in the sense that they are well-made, well-priced and do not need too much serious contemplation – wines for family meals, for easy, everyday drinking.

As well as the designation of many new appellation contrôlée zones – both a recognition and an encouragement of quality – the last 20 years has seen the classification of a large number of *vins de pays* – wines which recognize distinctly local traditions. Given the region's size and the number of its appellation contrôlée areas, there are inevitably more differences than similarities between the wines produced; but it is still possible to recognize certain stylistic groups.

As the driest and hottest part of France, the largest production by far is of red wine. From the Costières de Nîmes in the east to the tiny village of Collioure near the Spanish border, huge swathes of vineyard produce gutsy reds based on the Mediterranean grape varieties: Carignan, Grenache and Cinsaut – and on the superior or "noble" grapes, Syrah and Mourvèdre, whose homes are in the Rhône Valley and Provence. Carignan has traditionally been the most widely planted variety because it produces large quantities of grapes, regularly, for basic "plonk"; but others have more style and finesse: the Cinsault gives acidity and depth of colour, while the Syrah lends tannins and concentration and the Mourvèdre exotic perfumes of herbs, and tannins.

Quality varies, but less wildly than you might expect over such a large area. It is relatively easy to make reds in this climate, and the arrival of new technology, modern bottling lines and trained

▲ *There's no excuse for not knowing that Banyuls makes wine as you arrive at Port Vendres.*

winemakers has been sufficient to produce good reds from all the appellations – wines which bring out their juicy, peppery fruit with insouciant ease. This is particularly apparent in the more traditional areas of the Languedoc – Corbières and Minervois – where, quite suddenly, producers have started to create wines with forward, up-front fruit, almost New World in style – wines as suitable for today's barbecue as for *cassoulet*.

There are, of course, some areas producing wines which are generally of a better quality than others. The vineyards of the Hérault département – one of the most intensively planted wine regions of France – are home to Coteaux du Languedoc and the superior Coteaux du Languedoc-Villages, of which the villages of La Clape, Quatourze and Montpeyroux, are making perhaps the best.

The very best of the Midi's red wines are to be found in the south: the appellation of Saint-Chinian in the Hérault is revealing wines with much hitherto unsuspected elegance, while in the Aude département, just south, the twin appellations of Minervois and Corbières face each other across the Aude Valley – Minervois tending towards greater fruitiness, Corbières having spicy, wilder tastes which can be very exciting; both are for young drinking. The better cooperatives and individual estates are coming forward with well-made wines from these two large appellations, some of it aged in new oak barrels – which adds the complexity of spice and vanilla to the wine – but the reputation of the smaller appellation of Fitou, marketed as an inexpensive "gluggable" red wine, has suffered recently from over-production.

Baking in the sun, in the very driest part of France, are the wines of Côtes du Roussillon and Collioure, in the département of Pyrénées-Orientales. Languedoc and Roussillon share a history of over 2,000 years of viticulture and yet, despite physical closeness, their differences are

► *Vieux Banyuls, rich, sweet, Port-like wine aged in oak casks.*

quite marked, in climate and topography, Roussillon being hotter and more mountainous – and in the pronounced Catalan influence on the culture and cuisine of the south. Roussillon wines are different too, tending towards greater concentration and a raisiny taste from very ripe fruit; they are sometimes drier, and have, perhaps, a hint of the Spanish vanilla flavours from just across the frontier, lent by the oak casks used in maturing – allowing them to stand up to the pimentos, olives and vivid flavours of Catalan cooking.

Successful white wines are quite a recent phenomenon in the Midi, and relatively little is made in the established appellation contrôlée vineyards, leaving the new *vins de pays* areas as the source of white wines made from such grape varieties as Chardonnay and Sauvignon Blanc. These give fruity, fresh wines – perhaps lacking character a little, but always good value.

Modern winemaking techniques needed to be introduced before clean, fresh, white wines could be made in the Midi and, even now, many white wines, while clean, lack character and acidity, an inevitable result of the hot sun. Harvesting the grapes when they are under-ripe is one way of ensuring that they have acidity, and is a technique practised by the more go-ahead estates.

A very few appellations make white wine exclusively: Clairette de Bellegarde in the Gard makes fragrant wines (from the Clairette grape), but always with an underlying tendency to flabbiness. In neighbouring Hérault, Clairette du Languedoc makes heavier, more alcoholic wine, much of which is employed locally at the Noilly Prat plant to become good-quality vermouth, and is therefore not seen much outside the region.

Other dry white wines are found as part of many of the major appellations – Corbières, Minervois and Côtes du Roussillon – the Spanish Macabeo grape mixing happily with the French varieties: Picpoul, Clairette and Bourboulenc and giving a shot of acidity to the otherwise sometimes too full whites. This heavier style does, however, make a good partner for quite oily fish dishes such as sardines or tuna.

Given the climate, it is perhaps not surprising that the traditional white wine of the Midi should be sweet and alcoholic. The *vins doux naturels* made from the Muscat grape are found throughout the region, but certain small towns have established a pre-eminence in making these luscious, fortified white wines which appear as the regular local apéritif. The Hérault (producing Muscat de Frontignan, Muscat de Lunel, Muscat de Mireval and Muscat de Saint-Jean-de-Minervois) vies with Roussillon (producing Rivesaltes) as to which is best, but for my taste the lighter styles such as that found in Saint-Jean-de-Minervois or Lunel are more attractive, being fresher.

The other great fortified wine of the region is a

distinct oddity: a sweet red wine, made from the Grenache grape. Its nearest equivalent is Port; as with other sweet wines, it is drunk as an apéritif in France. A surprising amount of this red *vin doux naturel* is made outside any appellation, just for home consumption, but the Pyrénées-Orientales département in Roussillon is home to the finest of these wines.

Maury and Banyuls produce what are generally considered the best, because of their intensity, and Banyuls has, in addition, a style called Rancio: *vin doux naturel* aged for several years in barrels which are left exposed to the heat of summer and the cold of winter, a severe regime which results in a deliciously nutty, oxidized wine – an equivalent to Italy's *vin santo*.

One further wine style comes from the Midi, but this time from the coolest part of the region. Sparkling Blanquette de Limoux is said to have its origins in a tradition older than that of champagne. Produced in the high mountains south of Carcassonne in the Aude département, it gained its name not simply because it is a white wine, but from the white film that covers the underside of the Mauzac vines' leaves. Now there are moves to change its name to Crémant de Limoux, to emphasize its sparkling nature.

Languedoc and Roussillon are almost certainly the most exciting wine regions of France at the moment. Struggling to overcome years of neglect and over-production, to alter their once proud position as sponsors of a considerable proportion of the European "wine lake", producers have realized – quite suddenly it seems – that they do not have to make poor quality wine, fit only for distillation. By the proper selection of grape varieties, by concentrating on the vineyards in the hills, rather than on the heavy-yielding vineyards of the plains, and by investing in modern winemaking techniques and equipment to bring out fruit rather than flab, producers are revealing a range of exotic, vivid tastes rivalling those of Italy or Spain. Here is the region which is set fair to provide much of the best value drinking in Europe.

▼ *Château Saint-Auriol in the Corbières. The separate bush vines are typical of the region.*

LANGUEDOC AND ROUSSILLON

OTHER SPECIALITIES OF THE REGION AND WINES TO TRY WITH THEM

Languedoc looks in two directions for its culinary inspiration: to the mountains for its meat and cheese, and to the Mediterranean for its fish. To the south, Roussillon looks both to the Mediterranean and to Catalonia in Spain. The style of Languedoc's cuisine is more restrained, reflecting the region's past hardships, while Roussillon's cooking is full of life and colour. But if the two regions have a common theme, it is the use of olives and olive oil, of garlic and tomatoes, elements that recur time and again, giving rise to the term **à la languedocienne**, which refers to dishes cooked with tomatoes, aubergines, cep mushrooms and plenty of garlic.

Those ingredients reach their apogee in the simplest of dishes – and the strange-sounding names of some of these should not deter the culinary explorer; their names originate in the occitan language, the traditional dialect of southern France. **All y oli**, a paste of garlic, lemon and olive oil, is served either as a sauce or as an accompaniment to hors-d'oeuvre; **al pa ya all**, are croûtons rubbed with garlic, salt and olive oil; **all crémat**, is a mixture of bacon, red pimentos, olive oil and garlic, used to enliven soups, while **rouzole** is served with soup – a pancake of herby breadcrumbs and ham.

To drink: *a white from Clairette du Languedoc or Bellegarde, or one of the new, fresh style of white* vins de pays *wines is ideal with* all y oli. *With* all crémat *try a red Côtes du Roussillon. In its warmth, this wine is the closest in France to a Spanish-style wine.*

Fish naturally plays a large part in culinary life by the coast in both regions. There are shellfish – oysters and mussels come from the huge salt water lakes that break up the coast south of Montpellier. These are eaten raw or arrive in **pinyata roussillonaise**, Roussillon's version of *bouillabaisse*, the Provençal fish stew. Sardines are grilled, wine vinegar is added and they become **sardinada**. Anchovies – fresh or salted – crayfish stew, monkfish and tuna are all regular denizens of harbour-side restaurants.

To drink: *with sardines or anchovies a full, tannic red such as a Côtes du Roussillon or Corbières is best; with shellfish, try a dry Muscat from the Corbières.*

With cold fish, the traditional accompaniment is **beurre de Montpellier**: a rich, herby mixture containing shallots, garlic and egg.

Strangely, however, fish are rarely seen on tables far inland. Before many kilometres have been travelled, the emphasis is on meat. The star is the **cassoulet** (see recipes), but there is a curious tradition of pasties, **petits pâtés** – rather like Cornish pasties – which come from Béziers and Pézenas, north of Narbonne. These are filled with mutton and vegetables and eaten in the hand. **Daube** of beef

▲ *Anchovies are sold fresh or, for those inland, preserved in brine.*

(beef braised in red wine) and beef cooked with tomatoes, wine and olives, can tenderize and improve the flavour of poorer cuts. There are stews of haricot beans with pork, tomatoes and garlic – **estouffade de haricots blancs** – and soon, in Toulouse, you are in *foie gras* territory.

To drink: *beef casseroles and bean stews demand the rich, full-bodied reds of La Clape, Minervois or Corbières, preferably some of those where there is a hint of new wood in the taste, from the barrels in which the wine matured.*

Further inland again, as Mediterranean olives disappear, it is the turn of charcuterie: the famous **Toulouse sausage** of coarsely chopped pork, seasoned simply with salt and pepper or perhaps garlic, and hams from the

Montagne Noire – home still to wild boar. With colder winters, there is a need for hearty soups such as **soupe ariegoise**, based on chicken broth and filled out with ham and bread-crumbs, or **aillade toulousaine**, a broth flavoured with toast rubbed with garlic and olive oil. **Mourtayrol** is a saffron-flavoured soup. Beef, chicken, ham and vegetables are removed from the soup after cooking and served later; the stock is then cooked with bread and served first.

To drink: *any young red wine, perhaps even slightly chilled in the summer, would be suitable with the charcuterie.*

▲ *Olives and tomatoes: indispensable ingredients in the Midi.*

Down to the south, as Catalan flavours take over, it is the turn of snails, called locally cagaraoule, which, when barbecued over vine-cuttings with large quantities of garlic, become a dish known as **cargolade**.

To drink: *try a rich, full wine such as a Collioure or a Corbières*

Game birds from the Pyrenees mountain range are cooked **à la catalane**, with peppers and bitter Seville oranges; while lamb or mutton come braised **en pistache** in a gloriously pungent white wine sauce with garlic and pistachio nuts.

To drink: *with these Catalan dishes, drink a Côtes du Roussillon, or a Collioure, full of ripe, southern fruit.*

▼ *Artichokes, a local delicacy, come from Lozère in northern Languedoc.*

The hot climate of the summer lends itself to cold dishes. There are savoury tarts like the **feuilletés de collioure** from Roussillon, a puff pastry tartlet filled with tomatoes, anchovies and olives. Aubergines and red and green peppers turn up in salads with green beans, courgettes, and, particularly in Languedoc, chicory, artichoke and lettuce – all liberally doused with olive oil.

To drink: *a Vin de Pays Catalan; a wine with some tannin and acid is best.*

Fruit compotes are a favourite dessert – in fact anything fruit-based is popular, since there are so many luscious peaches, apricots, cherries and pears. But there is also a preference for sweeter foods which, it is said, dates from the Arab invasions of the Dark Ages. **Tourons**, honey and pistachio pastries, are regular delicacies found in pastry shops, while from Montpellier come **oreillettes de Montpellier**, fritters flavoured with lemon and rum. **Torteil** is an aniseed-flavoured *brioche* pastry from across the border in Catalonia; **rosquille** is an iced cake in a figure of eight. Castelnaudary, Carcassonne and Narbonne all have mouth-watering selections of sweet and sticky fancies.

To drink: *a honey and sweet grape tasting Muscat from Rivesaltes or Frontignan, or even a rich, matured Banyuls.*

Very little cheese is made in the region apart from goats' milk cheeses, of which the **Pélardons** from the Cévennes are the most famous. Small, thin and round they are sometimes rolled in herbs or black pepper. **Bleu de Loudes** is a strong-tasting cows' milk blue cheese.

To drink: *a Grenache-based sweet wine, such as a Banyuls.*

INDEX

Wines, grapes, wine-growers, appellations and references to a region's wine production are listed in bold; foods, dishes and culinary terms are given in italic. Figures in bold refer to recipes; figures in bold italic refer to photographs.

ACKNOWLEDGMENTS AND ADDRESSES

The following is a list of the hotels, restaurants, wine-growers, shops and food producers described in the preceding chapters that are open to the public. Other wine-growers and food producers, not listed here, may only be visited by appointment.

When telephoning from outside France, the number must be prefixed by your country's international dialling code and the digits 33.

Alsace

Wistub du Sommelier
51 Grand'Rue
68750 Bergheim
Telephone: 89 73 69 99

Bernard Antony
Maître Fromager Affineur
17 rue de la Montagne
Vieux-Ferrette
68480 Ferrette
Telephone: 89 40 42 22

Domaine Zind-Humbrecht
1 route de Colmar
68230 Turckheim
Telephone: 89 27 22 58

Sigmann Boucherie, Charcuterie
44 rue de la République
68040 Ingersheim
Telephone: 89 27 01 75

La Taverne Alsacienne
99 rue de la République
68040 Ingersheim
Telephone: 89 27 08 41

Christine Ferber
68230 Niedermorschwihr

Auberge de Brand
68230 Turckheim
Telephone: 89 27 06 10

Bordeaux and the Southwest

Le Lion d'Or
Place République
33460 Arcins
Telephone: 56 58 96 79

Château Loudenne
Saint-Yzans-de-Médoc
33340 Lesparre
Telephone: 56 09 05 03

Hôtel Le Relais des Landes
211 avenue Frédéric Bastiat
Rion-des-Landes
Telephone: 58 57 10 20

Burgundy

Château de Gilly
Gilly-les-Cîteaux
21640 Vougeot
Telephone: 80 62 89 98

Domaine Rossignol-Trapet
21220 Gevrey-Chambertin
Telephone: 80 51 87 26

Domaine de l'Arlot
Prémeaux-Prissey
21700 Nuits-Saint-Georges
Telephone: 80 61 27 11

La Cuverie
5 rue Chanoine-Donin
21420 Savigny-lès-Beaune
Telephone: 80 21 50 03

Champagne

Biscuit Fossier
44 boulevard Jamin
Rheims
Telephone: 26 07 27 56

Chocolaterie Deleans
20 rue Cérès
51100 Rheims
Telephone: 26 47 56 35

Aquatias Charcuterie
29 rue Roger Sondag
Ay
Telephone: 26 55 43 00

Les Délices de la Ferme
19 rue Saint-Thibault
51200 Epernay
Telephone: 26 55 30 18

Restaurant Le Mesnil-sur-Oger
2 rue Pasteur
51190 Le-Mesnil-sur-Oger
Telephone: 26 57 95 57

Restaurant Le Vigneron
Place Paul Jamot
51100 Rheims
Telephone: 26 47 00 71

Le Caveau
Rue Coopérative
51480 Cumières
Telephone: 26 54 83 23

La Touraine Champenoise
2 rue des Ponts
Tours-sur-Marne
Telephone: 26 58 91 93

Provence

La Cave
9 boulevard de la République
Cannes
Telephone: 93 99 79 87

Domaines Ott
22 boulevard d'Aguillon
06601 Antibes
Telephone: 93 34 38 91

Hôtel Bel-Air
06290 Saint-Jean-Cap-Ferrat
Telephone: 93 76 00 21

Hôtel Byblos
83990 Saint-Tropez
Telephone: 94 97 00 04

The Loire Valley

Marais Salants de Guérande
Pen-Bron
44350 Guérande
Telephone: 40 23 47 63

La Baguette
19 rue Paul Bellamy
44000 Nantes
Telephone: 40 48 15 20

Villa Mon Rêve
44115 Basse-Goulaine
Telephone: 40 03 55 50

Maison Gautier
9 rue Fosse
Nantes
Telephone: 40 48 23 19

Champignonnière du Saut aux Loups
Avenue de Saumur
49730 Montsoreau
Telephone: 41 51 70 30

L'Anguille Vagabonde
Place de l'Eglise
37500 Saint-Germain-sur-Vienne
Telephone: 47 95 96 48

Monsieur et Madame Guy Vazereau
La Roche Clermault

Hardouin Charcuterie
9 rue du Commerce
37210 Vouvray
Telephone: 47 52 73 37

Auberge de l'Ile
3 place Bouchard
37220 L'Ile Bouchard
Telephone: 47 58 51 07

Au Plaisir Gourmand
2 rue Parmentier
37500 Chinon
Telephone: 47 93 20 48

Languedoc and Roussillon

Monsieur Poudou
Moulin de Boysède
11220 Lagrasse
Telephone: 68 43 10 10

La Coopérative L'Olivbo
Bize
Telephone: 68 46 10 37

Monsieur et Madame Donnet
Villetritouls
11220 Lagrasse
Telephone: 68 24 04 95

Bernard et Jeannette Gaschard
Ferme de Carrus
Maironnes
11220 Lagrasse
Telephone: 68 43 12 37

La Horte
Restaurant à la Ferme
Rieux-en-Val
11220 Lagrasse
Telephone: 68 24 06 01

Conserverie Esquines
126 avenue Corbières
11700 Douzens
Telephone: 68 79 19 77

Restaurant Le Portanel
11100 Bages
Telephone: 68 42 81 66

Acknowledgments

All photographs for the book were specially commissioned from Joe Cornish and Richard McConnell.

Title Page: Joe Cornish; Introduction: Joe Cornish; Alsace: Joe Cornish (except Page 28, Richard McConnell); Bordeaux and the Southwest: Richard McConnell; Burgundy: Joe Cornish (except Page 73 bottom, Richard McConnell); Champagne: Joe Cornish; Provence: Joe Cornish; The Loire Valley: Richard McConnell (except Page 125 bottom, Joe Cornish); Languedoc and Roussillon: Richard McConnell (except Page 157 bottom, Joe Cornish).